CARETAKER CONVENTIONS IN AUSTRALASIA

MINDING THE SHOP FOR GOVERNMENT

CARETAKER CONVENTIONS IN AUSTRALASIA

MINDING THE SHOP FOR GOVERNMENT

JENNIFER MENZIES & ANNE TIERNAN

2nd edition

Centre for Governance and Public Policy
Griffith University

Australian
National
University

PRESS

Published by ANU Press
The Australian National University
Canberra ACT 0200, Australia
Email: anupress@anu.edu.au
This title is also available online at http://press.anu.edu.au

National Library of Australia Cataloguing-in-Publication entry

Author: Menzies, Jennifer, author.

Title: Caretaker conventions in Australasia : minding the shop for government /
                   Jennifer Menzies and Anne Tiernan.
                   2nd edition.

ISBN: 9781925021929 (paperback) 9781925021936 (ebook)

Subjects: Public administration--decision making.
                   Public administration--Australia.
                   Public administration--New Zealand.
                   Elections--Australia.
                   Elections--New Zealand.
                   Australia--Politics and government--21st century.
                   New Zealand--Politics and government--21st century.

Other Authors/Contributors:
                   Tiernan, Anne, 1968-, author.
                   Institute of Public Administration Australia.
                   Australia and New Zealand School of Government.

Dewey Number: 328.9

Cover design by Nic Welbourn and layout by ANU Press

Funding for this monograph series has been provided by the Australia and New Zealand School
of Government Research Program.

Contents

Author Profiles

Jennifer Menzies is a Director with the consultancy Policy Futures and a Commissioner with the Commonwealth Grants Commission. A former senior executive and Cabinet Secretary within the Queensland Department of the Premier and Cabinet, she has over 20 years' experience in both state and commonwealth governments. From 2007 to 2009 she was the inaugural Secretary for the Council for the Australian Federation. She consults in the field of public policy and governance and has published in the fields of caretaker conventions, federalism and intergovernmental relations. She is an Adjunct Senior Research Fellow with the Centre for Governance and Public Policy, Griffith University.

Anne Tiernan is an Associate Professor in the Centre for Governance and Public Policy at Griffith University. She is Director of postgraduate and executive programs in policy analysis and public administration in Griffith's School of Government and International Relations. A/Prof Tiernan's research interests include: policy advice, executive governance, policy capacity, federalism and intergovernmental coordination. She is author of several books including: *Lessons in Governing: A Profile of Prime Ministers' Chiefs of Staff* and *The Gatekeepers: Lessons from Prime Ministers' Chiefs of Staff* (both with R.A.W. Rhodes, Melbourne University Publishing, 2014), *Learning to be a Minister: Heroic Expectations, Practical Realities* (with Patrick Weller, Melbourne University Press, 2010) and *Power Without Responsibility: Ministerial Staffers in Australian Governments from Whitlam to Howard* (UNSW Press, 2007). A/Prof Tiernan is a member of the Member of the Public Records Review Committee of the Queensland State Archives and serves on the Board of Directors of St Rita's College Ltd. Between 2008 and 2012 she was a member of the Board of Commissioners of the Queensland Public Service Commission. A/Prof Tiernan consults regularly to Australian governments at all levels.

Acknowledgments

For an issue that so engages the attention of politicians and public servants for an intense period of about a month every couple of years, surprisingly little has been published on the topic of caretaker conventions. This monograph draws together that research, and the guidance documents developed by public service central agencies to address issues of practical concern in managing the business of government during an election campaign.

As we show in this second edition monograph, conventions are by nature, dynamic. They evolve through experience and political practice. This monograph addresses the theoretical underpinnings of the caretaker principles, traces their progressive institutionalisation in recent decades, and examines some contemporary challenges for their interpretation and observance. It is important to note however, that while our treatment of the guidance documents is currently accurate, they are 'live' documents that will adapt and change as experience and events dictate. It will therefore be necessary for practitioners and others with an interest in the trajectory of the caretaker conventions to monitor such changes and to consider them in the context of our arguments as laid out here.

Our research and understanding of the issues canvassed in this monograph has been assisted by the many Commonwealth, State, Territory and New Zealand officials who generously spoke to us about their experience of the caretaker conventions and reviewed sections of the manuscript.

We are grateful to Professor John Wanna of the ANZSOG research program, who engaged us to undertake this research with a practitioner audience in mind, and helped conceptualise and shape the manuscript. Special thanks to John Nethercote and Jonathan Boston for helpful comments on the first edition. For the second edition we would like to thank Suzie Aron, Clara Marsh and Emilie Barton for research assistance and Susan Jarvis for her careful and helpful copy editing assistance. Special thanks to James Boyle for his industrious and creative pursuit of documents and recent trends in New Zealand and local government.

Anne Tiernan and Jennifer Menzies
September 2014

Foreword to the Second Edition

This revised, highly successful monograph on caretaker conventions by Jennifer Menzies and Anne Tiernan updates their substantial review of the rules and conventions applying in the lead-up to elections across the many Australasian jurisdictions. The first edition was published by ANZSOG in 2007. It pioneered research work into this area and provided a much-needed comparative assessment of conventions and protocols in caretaker periods. Their original 2007 edition was then the ninth research monograph in the ANZSOG series with ANU Press; and this one appears now when the ANZSOG series of research monographs numbers some 40 titles – ranging from studies of policy issues and redesign, public management, performance and implementation studies, integrity and accountability analyses, and fundamental aspects of good governance. The entire series is available under the ANZSOG monograph series at http://press.anu.edu.au/titles/australia-and-new-zealand-school-of-government-anzsog-2/.

As these authors suggest, observed protocols and ethical standards of behaviour at times of elections (or in the immediate wake of elections if results are unclear) are important to the fabric and integrity of our democratic system. Caretaker conventions clarify decision-making roles and responsibilities, and provide confidence in the wider political system that governments cannot inappropriately make executive decisions at the termination of their parliamentary term. They guard against out-going governments improperly using executive powers to advantage their electoral prospects, and prevent them from taking partisan decisions with longer term consequences to which their main political challengers might not wish to commit. These conventions also serve to protect the apolitical and professional nature of our various public services, ensuring they are well-placed to serve whichever party wins the ensuing election, as well as ensuring that any new incoming government has maximum capacity to pursue its mandate without being unduly constrained by decisions taken immediately before the election.

Internal guidance has long been available to public servants working for Australian and New Zealand governments but such guidance has not been so widely available at the state and local government levels. This revised monograph provides a state of the art guidance on appropriate professional standards for those working at all levels of government in Australia and New Zealand.

ANZSOG would like to acknowledge the involvement of the Institute of Public Administration Australia as an initial co-sponsor of this research and continues to look forward to cooperating on further monographs that promote high standards in public administration.

Professor John Wanna
National Research Director
Australia and New Zealand School of Government
20 May 2014

List of Acronyms and Abbreviations

AAP	Australian Associated Press
ABC	Australian Broadcasting Corporation
ACT	Australian Capital Territory
AFP	Australian Federal Police
AGIMO	Australian Government Information Management Office
ALP	Australian Labor Party
APS	Australian Public Service
APSC	Australian Public Service Commission
CEO	Chief Executive Officer
CMC	Crime and Misconduct Commission (Qld)
COAG	Council of Australian Governments
Cth	Commonwealth
DPM&C	Department of Prime Minister and Cabinet (Australia)
JSCER	Joint Select Committee on Electoral Reform
MMP	Mixed Member Proportional
MOU	Memorandum of Understanding
MPs	Members of Parliament
NBN Co	National Broadband Network Company
NSWDPC	New South Wales Department of Premier and Cabinet
NZDPM&C	New Zealand Department of Prime Minister and Cabinet
NZSSC	New Zealand State Services Commission
PBO	Parliamentary Budget Office
SADPC	South Australian Department of Premier and Cabinet
SAS	Special Air Service
WADPC	Western Australian Department of Premier and Cabinet
US	United States

1. Introduction

Despite the regular cycle of elections in Australia and New Zealand, the application of the caretaker conventions remains a continuing source of conflict and media attention. In 2013, the federal election provided a rich source of controversy, as have recent state and territory elections. During the course of these campaigns, incumbent governments were accused of breaching 'caretaker conventions' — the principles and practices that guide the conduct of ministers and officials during an election campaign.

Caretaker conventions have evolved as a check on executive power in circumstances where there is no parliament to which it can be held accountable. They are observed during an election period, in a situation where, for example, a government has lost the support of the legislature, or where there is a delay in forming a government after an election. Although the business of government continues, because of the potential for a change of government, caretaker arrangements require that no new policy decisions be taken, no major contracts be entered into and no significant appointments be made. Caretaker conventions are based on shared understandings of how politicians should behave: they are not law and are not adjudicated by the courts.

The federal election on September 7, 2013 was a bitter contest between the minority Labor government, led by the recently reinstalled Prime Minister Kevin Rudd, and the Coalition parties under the leadership of Tony Abbott. The election date was initially settled by Prime Minister Julia Gillard in January 2013, when she announced the date of September 14. This raised some controversy about when the caretaker period would start, despite the conventions only applying after the dissolution of the House of Representatives. The reappointment of Kevin Rudd as Prime Minister saw him reclaim his prerogative to announce the timing of the federal election at his own choosing.

The extended unofficial campaign, as well as the five-week official campaign, led to a number of Opposition complaints, with claims that caretaker conventions had been breached by the following:

- *Signing international agreements.* The handling of asylum seekers during the election campaign was hotly contested by both sides. Opposition Leader Tony Abbott initially complained about the signing of a Memorandum of Understanding (MOU) between Australia and Papua New Guinea on 5 August 2013 on the transfer and resettlement of asylum seekers. Because the agreement was signed the day before the dissolution of the Parliament — though a day after the announcement of the election — the Secretary of the Department of the Prime

Minister and Cabinet (DPM&C) advised the Opposition Leader that 'the Department considers the validity of the MOU is not affected by the commencement of the caretaker period' (Watt 2013a).

- *Government advertising campaigns* — notably saturation television, radio and print advertising for the 'No Boat, No Visa' campaign. This campaign was controversial before the commencement of the caretaker period, and the Opposition Leader refused to agree to the onshore component of this advertising campaign continuing because he believed it 'was being used purely for partisan political purposes' (Abbott 2013a). The withdrawal of the Opposition's consent to continue to run the advertisements meant the government was in contravention of the caretaker guidelines, which state 'bipartisan agreement is sought for campaigns that are to continue' and campaigns which 'are a matter of contention between the parties are normally discontinued' (DPM&C 2013). The government counteracted by claiming the government was only required to 'consult' with the Opposition, and such consultation had occurred (*The Drum*, 20 August 2013). For a case study on this controversy, see Chapter 5.

- *Departmental costings of Opposition commitments.* Two weeks before the election, Prime Minister Kevin Rudd made a statement that the government had found a $10 billion hole in the savings claimed by the Coalition. Rudd said the costings hole was based on figures from the Commonwealth Treasury, the Department of Finance and Deregulation and the Parliamentary Budget Office. That day, the Secretaries of Treasury and Finance issued a joint statement denying they had undertaken costings of Opposition policies. This highly unusual intervention by senior officials was forced upon them to protect the impartiality of the Commonwealth public service, and to prevent the perception these departments were modelling Opposition policies on behalf of the government during an election campaign.

These controversies highlight the many challenges facing the public service during election campaigns. Public officials can apply the caretaker guidelines, but their recommendations do not have to be adopted by the government. They do not have the power to enforce the observance of the conventions. This responsibility sits with ministers, the Prime Minister or the Premier. Public servants are also under pressure to maintain impartiality and, just as importantly, the perception of impartiality. Oppositions are constantly alert in looking to identify any advantage they believe the incumbent government could be receiving during the caretaker period.

Allegations can flow both ways, with ministers complaining that shadow ministers have also misused the conventions relating to consultation between the Opposition and the public service in the pre-election period. Specifically, they have expressed concerns that requests for information from government departments and agencies have been used as a basis for political attacks rather than as part of their legitimate preparation for government.

Complaints of breaches of caretaker conventions during elections are not new. What has arguably changed is a more adversarial political context which has made these complaints more frequent and bitter, with the conflict aggravated through media coverage. Although such complaints rarely gain much popular traction, they pose significant difficulties for public servants, who are expected to walk the line of impartiality in the heated and intensely partisan atmosphere of an election campaign.

Recent examples of alleged breaches offer interesting insights into some of the challenges of applying and interpreting caretaker conventions, and raise questions about:

- the nature and status of caretaker conventions
- when they apply
- some of the forces affecting their nature and observance
- the consequences that new modes of regulation and oversight have for the interpretation and adjudication of the actions of key actors during the caretaker period
- the future of caretaker conventions, given pressures on their adjudication and interpretation.

These questions are explored in the second edition of *Caretaker Conventions in Australasia*. This edition builds on the observations of the 2007 edition as it explores the difficulties faced by public servants in both updating and applying caretaker conventions. The monograph is based on a detailed exploration of the most recently published caretaker conventions and includes insights from interviews with senior government officials experienced in managing during the caretaker period. This analysis highlights the dilemmas associated with codifying and formalising practices that derive from shared understandings about what constitutes 'appropriate' political behaviour. It also exposes a fundamental transformation in their scope and intent.

Historically, caretaker conventions were developed as simple guidances for ministers, reminding them of the need to moderate their conduct during the election period because of the lack of an operating parliament to which they were accountable. Over time, responsibility for maintaining and updating the guidance documents has been taken over by the bureaucracy. As a result, the focus of guidance documents has shifted from an emphasis on ministerial restraint to one of supporting bureaucratic decision-making in uncertain times. This has added complexity to the guidances, with the result that they have become documents that perform dual and potentially irreconcilable functions: seeking to provide, on the one hand, guidelines about what constitutes appropriate political behaviour and, on the other, advice aimed at protecting the bureaucracy from controversy and claims of partisanship.

The crafting and updating of documents by public servants has added detail on issues primarily of concern to the bureaucracy. The traditional purpose of the guidance documents has become conflated with bureaucratic attempts to shield public servants from potentially inappropriate ministerial demands for responsiveness during an election campaign. One commentator has observed that caretaker conventions are a good example of A.F. Davies' claim that Australians have a particular 'talent for bureaucracy' (quoted in Colebatch 2005). Instead of ministers being required to act responsibly during an election campaign, the onus is now on how the bureaucracy deals with ministerial requests, as well as access to, and use of, government infrastructure.

This subtle shift of emphasis from the behaviour of ministers to public servants has created additional constraints on the activities of public administration during the caretaker period. For example, the original intent of the guidance *not* to undertake significant appointments in the caretaker period was directed towards governments, and was aimed at deterring them from 'stacking' boards and statutory authorities with sympathetic appointees — particularly if they were in danger of losing office. Although guidance was aimed at major appointments — meaning appointments in which a minister has a role (usually statutory appointments) — some jurisdictions now provide advice to administrators on limiting the appointment of senior bureaucrats, including down to mid-levels.

Anxious to avoid criticism and controversy, public officials sometimes choose to constrain their administrative prerogatives, even in areas that are not subject to ministerial oversight or intervention under normal circumstances. The dual nature of the conventions has led to continuing confusion over where responsibility lies in preventing breaches, and who should enforce the conventions. Is it the role of the public service to patrol the boundaries of acceptable ministerial behaviour or should responsibility for observing the conventions lie primarily with ministers? Given the inherent dilemmas of the caretaker period, there has been an increasing tendency to codify and formalise guidance on the caretaker conventions. As the comparative overview of caretaker arrangements in Appendix A of this monograph demonstrates, there is significant policy transfer and learning between jurisdictions, although there are local differences in the application of caretaker principles based on local controversies.

Of course, elections are a fraught time for public administrators in Westminster-style political systems. For the duration of the 'caretaker period' — the period between the calling of an election and the return of the existing government or the commissioning of a new government — public servants must tread a careful line. In particular, they must be seen to be apolitical: although they may be required to brief the government's political opponents, they must maintain the policy status quo and ensure administrative continuity until the election result is known. In this context, they must administer policy, provide advice and manage programs in a highly charged and adversarial political environment in which key actors — ministers, ministerial staff, shadow ministers, the Opposition, its staff and journalists — can be expected to have varying degrees of familiarity and appreciation of the application (and nuances) of the practices and procedures developed to regulate how a government should operate once an election is called.

Paradoxically, the application of the caretaker conventions becomes enormously significant, if only for a short period of time, every three or four years. For the vast majority of public sector employees this means they only have a sporadic and limited contact with the conventions and, at any election, many officers are working in a caretaker environment for the first time.

This monograph collects that knowledge, and explores some of the judgements that public sector employees might be required to make, in order to provide a comprehensive overview of the principles and practice of caretaker conventions in Australian and New Zealand jurisdictions. It examines what our caretaker conventions are, where they originated and how they have evolved, and includes a glossary of key terms and concepts. Using cases and examples from recent elections, it explores some of the pressures on the interpretation and management of caretaker conventions. This ANZSOG monograph collates and consolidates current guidance documents on the caretaker period, and presents a comparative analysis of caretaker arrangements as they stand in Australian Commonwealth, state, territory and local government jurisdictions, and in New Zealand. The monograph addresses issues of practical concern to politicians in both government and Opposition, as well as to public servants, to assist them in management during the caretaker period. It aims to demystify and critically assess many of the practices that have evolved over time.

2. What are Conventions?

Australia's political system is founded on the principle of 'responsible government'. Its basic tenets are that, subject to the Constitution, Parliament is supreme; the government is responsible to Parliament; ministers have to be in Parliament; regular elections will be held; and there is a professional bureaucracy that is independent of but accountable to ministers. Unlike the United Kingdom, Australia has a written Constitution, and some of these principles are captured in that document.[1] The provisions of the Constitution comprise the formal rules of government. But formal rules are only part of the story about how a system of government operates. In areas about which the Constitution is silent, political behaviour is guided by 'well established practice, methods, habits, maxims and usages' — many of them long-standing — which were inherited from colonial parliaments, which in turn inherited them from Westminster. It is these practices, methods and usages that tend to be referred to as 'conventions of the Constitution' (Reid 1977, p. 244).

Conventions have become an integral part of Westminster-style democracies, filling in the detail and helping political practice to adhere to the principles of responsible government (Heard 1991, p. 1). For example, conventions cover:

- rules about the relationship between the Prime Minister or Premier and Cabinet
- the role of Cabinet
- relations between the Crown and the Parliament
- relations between the two Houses of Parliament (Marshall 1984, p. 4)[2]
- how budgets are appropriated
- ceremonial etiquette and protocols (for example, both the Prime Minister and Leader of the Opposition are represented at major events, funerals, openings and military parades during the caretaker period).

New Zealand conventions also rest on a mixture of written and unwritten constitutional precepts. McLeay (1999, p. 12) reports that:

> The conduct of a caretaker government, for example, is guided by: the *Constitution Act 1986* (which defines, among other things, the tenure of Ministers); the core convention that Parliament is sovereign and that governments must command the confidence of the House ...

---

1 Proposals to formally include some aspects of responsible government in the written Constitution were formally rejected during the constitutional debates before federation (Rhodes et al. 2009, Ch. 3).

2 Standing Orders of the Commonwealth Parliament are the rules and orders made by each House under section 50 of the Constitution concerning, inter alia, the order and conduct of business and proceedings. They also cover the 'mode in which its power, privileges and immunities may be exercised and upheld'.

Various definitions exist regarding what constitutes a constitutional convention. Most definitions refer to the early work of British scholars A.V. Dicey and Sir Ivor Jennings, who investigated the differences between the law of the Constitution and the conventions of the Constitution (Heard 1991, p. 4). Jennings (1959, p. 159) famously identified three questions to be asked as the precondition to the existence of a convention. Firstly:

- what are the precedents?

- secondly, did the actors in the precedents believe they were bound by a rule?

- and thirdly, is there a good reason for the rule?

For Jaconelli (2005, p. 151), conventions are 'social rules that possess a constitutional — and not merely a political — significance'. He argues that emphasising their social nature captures two of their fundamental features: their normative quality in prescribing standards of behaviour, and the fact that they are not enforced in the courts. Their specific constitutional character 'bears out, in addition, the role that they play, akin to that performed by written (and legally enforceable) constitutions in allocating power and controlling the manner of its exercise as between the organs of government and political parties' (Jaconelli 2005, pp. 151–2). The nature of conventions and their relationships to the law is highly contested. It is not our intention to rehearse the various debates here. A useful summary can be found in Marshall (2004, pp. 37–44).

Conventions arise in several ways: through practice acquiring a strong obligatory character over time and/or through the explicit agreement of the relevant actors (Heard 1991, p. 10). As an example of the latter, Sampford (1987, p. 386) cites the former convention dating from 1952 on the filling of Australian Senate vacancies with a member of the same political party. The question of whether this was, in fact, a convention, was hotly contested, although it had been established practice since 1952. Controversy over the 'breaching' of this convention by the New South Wales government in 1975,[3] and by the Queensland government later the same year,[4] was the catalyst for an amendment to section 15 of the Constitution in 1977 to specify more clearly how casual Senate vacancies should be dealt with by state parliaments.[5]

---

3   A joint sitting of the NSW Parliament chose an independent, Cleaver Bunton, to replace outgoing Labor Senator Lionel Murphy, who resigned when he was appointed to the High Court of Australia.

4   Queensland Premier Joh Bjelke-Petersen nominated the anti-Whitlam Pat Field for the vacancy created by the death of Labor Senator Bert Milliner. Both appointments undermined the ALP government's tenuous hold on the Senate, setting the scene for its dismissal in November 1975. As it happened, Bunton voted with the government in the crucial votes; Field did not vote at all as his selection was challenged and referred to a Court of Disputed Returns.

5   For guidance on the current practice for the filling of casual vacancies, see Odgers' *Australian Senate Practice*, 12th edition.

Marshall (1984, p. 8) notes that conventions arise from 'a series of precedents that are agreed to have given rise to a binding rule of behaviour'. Alternatively, a convention may derive from some 'acknowledged principle of government which provides a reason or justification for it' (Marshall 1984, p. 9). In practice, conventions may be confirmed after the event. He observes that many conventions are negative in form — connoting that political actors should constrain their behaviour or refrain from certain courses of action.

A key characteristic of conventions is their flexibility. Since they are not subject to judicial interpretation, they evolve in response to changing circumstances and political values. This lack of legal definition permits 'the adaptation of constitutional rules to changes in the general political principles and values of the day, without the need for formal amendment to existing positive law' (Cooray 1979, p. 5). Rhodes et al. (2009, p. 60) note that Australian politicians have consistently rejected proposals to codify many constitutional conventions, preferring to rely instead on the resilient and evolving traditions of responsible government.[6]

Morality, obligation and reciprocity

Conventions have been described by Marshall (1984) as the 'critical morality' of the Constitution. They impose a series of obligations that are morally and politically binding rather than legally imposed (Marshall 1984, p. 17). The courts can recognise the existence of conventions and refer to them in judicial interpretation of laws, but they are not enforceable through the legal system.[7] They operate as a normative force for political actors to conduct themselves in specific ways (Jaconelli 2005, p. 151). Political actors recognise and abide by conventions because 'they are believed to formulate valid rules of obligation' (Marshall, cited in Jaconelli 2005, p. 150), and they are regarded by all sides of politics as useful and generally worth observing. They are observed because political actors find them helpful and functional. For example, it is generally accepted that responsible parliamentary government in Australia is underpinned by adherence to a number of key conventions, including:

- governments recognise a loyal Opposition
- ministers must answer for their departments or provide explanations if questioned

---

6   For a discussion of efforts to formalise and codify key conventions of the Australian Constitution, see Sampford (1987).
7   See, for example, Marshall (2004, pp. 38–42); Heard (1991); Twomey and Withers (2007).

- ministers must not mislead Parliament — or, if they do so inadvertently, they must correct the record immediately

- ministers should attend Question Time unless urgent business prevents them from doing so.

For a convention to exist, actors must be aware of an obligation to behave in particular ways, and believe they are bound to adhere to its prescriptions. If this occurs, then the continuation of the practice of adhering to the convention remains high. Agreement and acceptance are important considerations in this context, as are expectations of reciprocity and mutuality. As Jaconelli (2005, p. 171) notes: the party that is in power at the moment respects the constraints that are imposed on it by constitutional conventions in the expectation that the Opposition parties, when they attain office, will likewise respect the same constraints.

The observance of conventions forms a restraint on the abuse of power by the government or the Crown (Hood Phillips and Jackson 1978, p. 108). For example, the application of caretaker conventions during an election campaign formalises the rights of the Opposition as a potential future government, and voluntarily restrains the governing party from exploiting the advantages of incumbency. Adherence to conventions can be seen as a constitutional compact of 'mutual forbearance', where each party, as it gains government, is schooled in the discipline of observing the constraints imposed by conventions (Jaconelli 2005, p. 173).

A further safeguard to observance of constitutional conventions in the Australian and New Zealand context is the role of the Governor-General. Hasluck (1979, p. 12) argues that the Governor-General 'occupies a position where he can help ensure that those who conduct the affairs of the nation do so strictly in accordance with the Constitution and the laws of the Commonwealth and with due regard to the public interest'. According to Hasluck (1979, p. 18), because of the Governor-General's close and regular contact with ministers through Executive Council, the Governor-General 'is both a watchdog over the Constitution and laws for the nation as a whole and a watchdog for the government considered as a whole (whatever government may be in power)'.

Moral sanctions against continued and deliberate breaches include the diminution of the system of government as a whole and the loss of 'respect for the established distribution of authority' (Marshall and Moodie 1971, p. 32). Breaches diminish the power of the convention and the loss of restraint on the abuse of power undermines the principle of reciprocity and mutuality that underpins the adherence to conventions.

It is generally accepted that the main sanction against the abuse of conventions is political. Dicey (1959, p. 444) argues that the power of public opinion ensures obedience. Ongoing media and public scrutiny of political behaviour ensures that breaches are well publicised by journalists, commentators and the Opposition. It has been observed that where a 'breach' of a convention is likely to be politically costly, the convention is far more secure (Sampford 1987, p. 375). However, voter cynicism and disengagement from politics raise questions about whether political sanctions are a sufficient deterrent to a breach of conventions. Sometimes, concerns that conventions have been breached reveal a complainant's lack of familiarity with the nature and status of conventions rather than a deliberate substantive breach (as, for instance, occurred with the Bjelke-Petersen calculation).

The application of conventions relies on judgement, knowledge of precedents and a desire to see the continuation and upholding of the convention. It is this exercise of prudence that creates uncertainty for many politicians and bureaucrats, since interpretation is inevitably subjective, situational and context-dependent. However, the application of conventions remains critical to adhering to the Westminster principles of responsible government.

3. Origins of Caretaker Conventions

The source of a convention is frequently difficult to trace because of the lack of either an authoritative text or an established authority to issue or adjudicate conventions (Sampford 1987, p. 369). Most of the conventions guiding political life in Australia and New Zealand derive from the Westminster tradition, and the logic of parliamentary government (Davis et al. 2001, p. 12; Rhodes et al. 2009, pp. 5–9).

Turning specifically to caretaker conventions, these guide the conduct of governments and the bureaucracy during election periods (until a new government is sworn in)[1] or in circumstances where, for example, a government has lost its parliamentary majority. These conventions ensure that somebody has a 'hold of the formal levers of power until a new government can be formed' (Laver and Shepsle 1994, pp. 291–2). Boston et al. (1998, p. 631) note that while periods of caretaker government occur in all parliamentary democracies, they tend to be both more frequent and more protracted in countries with proportional representation because election outcomes are often less clear cut, and the need to form coalition or minority governments can cause significant delays.

Within Westminster systems, caretaker conventions sit within a sub-set of conventions about the accountability of the elected government to Parliament (Marshall 1984, p. 18). Rhodes and Weller (2005, p. 2) note that the Westminster model comprises 'a set of beliefs and a shared inheritance that creates expectations and hands down rules that guide and justify behaviour'. The belief that the party in opposition is an alternative executive-in-waiting, and therefore entitled to a smooth transition to office should voters award it an electoral majority, is fundamental. This belief is lent weight by the progressive institutionalisation of the Opposition's role through entitlements (and, in some cases, salaries) for shadow ministers and office-holders, the provision of staff, specific arrangements in the Standing Orders and so on. Caretaker conventions moderate the substantial advantages of incumbency by constraining the power of the political executive during the election campaign and until a new government is appointed. They provide guidance to ministers, the Opposition and public servants about how the business of government should be conducted during the caretaker period.

---

1   This is usually a matter of a few days in two-party majoritarian systems like Australia, but can take longer if no party enjoys a clear majority. In New Zealand under MMP, the process of government formation following recent elections has taken approximately two weeks, with nine weeks (after the first MMP election in 1996) being the longest so far.

Broadly, caretaker conventions specify the following during the caretaker period:

- Governments should avoid making major policy decisions that are likely to commit an incoming government — the government and the public service should thus maintain the policy 'status quo' (Boston et al. 1998).

- Governments should also avoid making significant appointments or signing major contracts.

- Governments should not include public servants in election activities.

Like the other types of conventions discussed above, caretaker conventions have evolved to add detail to the administrative practices derived from the Constitution. In common with other aspects of the Westminster tradition, they adapt to reflect changing practices and political mores. They have evolved through experience, from observation of practices elsewhere and on the basis of advice from constitutional experts and commentators, political leaders and the Cabinet Office (McLeay 1999, p. 12). This means the application of the conventions is simultaneously both simple and complex. The application of conventions is in some ways simple, because they are based on two principles:

- With the dissolution of the House, there is no popular chamber to which the Executive government can be responsible.

- Every general election brings with it the possibility of a change of government. (DPM&C 1987, p. 39)

Applying the conventions can also be complex because difficult judgements sometimes have to be made about whether an action will cause a breach of those underlying principles. Unlike laws, the interpretation of which can be tested in courts, conventions reflect the beliefs and practices of political actors — their interpretation is fluid, often contested and subject to a dynamic and constantly evolving political environment. New challenges or technical possibilities — such as the use of the departmental internet by the incumbent party — can arise during an election campaign. The administration of caretaker conventions depends on a body of corporate knowledge about past application combined with sound judgement to deal with new issues as they arise.

The highly charged atmosphere of general elections in Australia and New Zealand means that caretaker conventions have not been without their controversies. Debate generally has been around their application in specific circumstances rather than the fundamentals of the principles that define them. The evolution of caretaker conventions in these two countries has focused on increasing detail on 'guidance' on how to apply them. Challenges to their application during an election campaign have led to further additions to formal guides about their application in order to clarify and remove existing ambiguities. The intention is not to change the 'rules' but rather to reduce breaches by a more precise statement of the application (Sampford 1987, p. 373).

Breaches and sanctions in the caretaker period

Claimed breaches of caretaker conventions are a mainstay of election campaigns. In Australia, responsibility for the administration of the caretaker conventions rests with the Prime Minister, the Premier or the Chief Minister, who is required to 'self-police' the rules (Jaconelli 2005, p. 176). Self-policing is not always the preferred option for an Opposition that suspects a breach of the conventions by those in power. In the heat of an election campaign, an Opposition is understandably reluctant to have the leader of the party it is challenging arbitrating on complaints about its own behaviour. Because the conventions are not legally binding, a disgruntled complainant has only two types of sanctions upon which to call —moral sanctions or political sanctions.

Alleged breaches of caretaker conventions during an election campaign revolve around the perception that the government has benefited from using the resources of office to give it an unfair advantage over the Opposition (see, for example, McMullan 2007, pp. 27–31). The weight of public condemnation may be sufficient to embarrass and politically damage the government for the perceived breach, especially if the issue is taken up vigorously by the media. The intention is to harm the political capital of the government by showing its moral deficiency and inability to be trusted with handling the delicate niceties of government.

It would be true to say that almost every election sees a public skirmish about an alleged breach of the caretaker conventions. It is now part of the political grist of election tactics and an area in which both the media and voters find it hard to discern the credibility of the complaints. It remains difficult to resolve these allegations because decisions are based on fine judgements about the applicability of the conventions in each particular circumstance. The lack of an authoritative mediation process means that it can never be ascertained whether a violation has in fact occurred (Jaconelli 2005, p. 163).

One area that has received little attention is the accusation of a breach against a public servant. Ironically, the sanctions for a breach by the bureaucracy are more real and enforceable than the moral or political sanctions applying to politicians. Public servants are bound by their relevant Codes of Conduct, which include the need to act 'impartially'.[2] This is reinforced by the penalties in *Public Service Acts* that allow for termination and other sanctions if the Code of Conduct is breached. This means if a public servant is found to have acted partially during an election campaign — even if they did so under the direction of the minister — it amounts to misconduct and is grounds for disciplinary action. The stakes for public servants to maintain the caretaker conventions during an election period are higher than for their political masters.

This has led to increased documentation, the development of guidance documents for governments and especially greater involvement of the public service to explain and assist with decision-making during this time. The next section identifies and explores the elements that make up the caretaker conventions of the Commonwealth and New Zealand governments, the Australian states, territories and local government jurisdictions.

Caretaker conventions: Guidelines and application

Australia

Although there is evidence of earlier informal acceptance of the need for caution during the caretaker period (Wilson 1995), the first public record of caretaker conventions in Australia is in the form of a letter from Prime Minister Robert Menzies to his ministers at the outset of the 1951 double dissolution elections, stating:

> I should also be glad if you would note that whilst continuing to take whatever action you deem necessary in connection with the ordinary administration of your Department, you should not make decisions on matters of policy or those of a contentious nature without first referring the matter to myself. (quoted in DPM&C 1987, p. 40)

By 1961, the established practice was for the Prime Minister to write to all ministers advising them explicitly of the need to avoid 'major policy decisions or important appointments' in the relevant period (DPM&C 1987). The ball was firmly in the ministers' court, it being their responsibility to behave accordingly.

---

2   It should be noted that the obligation on public servants to observe and demonstrate impartiality is not specific to the caretaker period, and is relevant at any time. However, in the caretaker period when political sensitivities are heightened, the risk of perceived partiality may be greater. Public servants might reasonably be expected to promote government policy in normal times. In a caretaker period, however, this might be seen as promoting the government rather than the policy.

The need for more detailed guidance — particularly on consultations with the Opposition — became relevant when, after two decades of Coalition government, the 1969 election raised the prospect of a change of government. In the event, three more years would elapse before it became a reality. The 1972 election saw the public service confront a transition for the first time in 23 years.

Former Governor-General Sir Paul Hasluck added to the sparse material on caretaker conventions by identifying what he thought was the key intent of the convention in his Queale Memorial Lecture in 1972:

> no new decisions on matters of major policy should be taken and no appointments to high office should be made. The common sense of this convention is to avoid a situation in which an expiring government may do something, which a month or so later, an incoming government may immediately try to cancel. The philosophy of it is that if a question on major policy is being put to the electorate at an election, a government should not make final decisions on that question before the electorate has given its answer. (Hasluck 1979, p. 18)

In 1983 and 1985, the Constitutional Conventions — meetings of Commonwealth, state and local government politicians — sought to codify and declare the conventions guiding the Australian political system.[3] Resolution 32, adopted at the 1983 meeting, is based on the Hasluck pronouncement (Lindell 1988, p. 322), and is the only resolution on the caretaker convention. It states:

> No important new initiative is taken, and no appointment to high office is made, by a government in the period immediately prior to a general election for the House of Representatives unless it can be publicly justified as necessary in the national interest. (*Proceedings of the Australian Constitutional Convention* 1983)

Marshall (2004, p. 42) notes that, unlike the courts, the Australian Convention:

> had no particular hold on the public imagination or claim to deference and it is unclear what the effect or significance of promulgating a declaration of this kind can be. Unless or until the committee's conclusions are embodied in legislation (when they would cease to be conventions), there seems no very good reason for anyone to defer to the views of such a body.

The Governor-General can require additional restrictions during an election campaign, but these are rare, with the only Australian example related to the

---

3   This process was not uncontroversial, with debate about the necessity, membership, authority and impact on the nature of conventions on the 'recognise and declare' model. See Sampford (1987) for a detailed examination of this process of codification.

double-dissolution elections in 1975 when the 'caretaker Prime Minister', Malcolm Fraser — appointed after the Whitlam government was sacked — gave specific undertakings to then Governor-General Sir John Kerr that no appointments or dismissals would be made and no policies would be initiated (DPM&C 1987, p. 40). More usually, the Governor-General's role in caretaker arrangements might be exercised through Executive Council. Hasluck (1979, p. 18) gives a flavour of this potential in the following observation:

> Of course the business of the country cannot be wholly suspended and there may be emergencies in which action should be taken at once, but, if a single Minister overlooks the convention, it is customary to defer his recommendation and draw the attention of the Prime Minister to the fact so that it becomes a matter for the Prime Minister or his Cabinet to decide whether the urgency is so great that action must be taken at once.

Documentation and guidance

The conventions were gradually refined over the years (Codd 1996, p. 23). The first detailed text of their intent and application was published in 1987 as a special article in the Department of Prime Minister and Cabinet's *Annual Report 1986–87*. Noting the relative lack of written material on the conventions, it reflected 'the Department's experience in relation to the conventions and associated practices, arising from its advisory and coordinating role' (DPM&C 1987, p. 39). Arguably, it indicates that the imperative for clarifying caretaker arrangements had shifted from the realm of the political (guidance to ministers about what they could and should do) to the administrative. It also means that political conventions have become 'legalistic', with lawyers increasingly brought in to administer or comment on them.

It has been noted that conventions evolve with political practice and reflect prevailing mores. In addition, we can state that formal guidance on their application has increased significantly in Australian jurisdictions since the 1980s. A major review and consolidation of the existing caretaker arrangements was undertaken by the Department of the Prime Minister and Cabinet (DPM&C) after the 1987 election. A significant addition was a set of *Guidelines for Pre-Election Consultation with Officials* by the Opposition. The issue of what kind of contact should be allowed between public servants and the alternative government had been bubbling since the 1970s. Whitlam had unsuccessfully sought permission from then Prime Minister William McMahon to meet with public servants prior to the 1972 election to discuss the administrative implications of Labor's policies (Hawker and Weller 1974, p. 100).

Thereafter, a summary of the guidance on caretaker conventions, with an emphasis on Cabinet matters, was incorporated into the *Cabinet Handbook*.

At less than two pages, it is far less detailed than the DPM&C guidance document (which now runs to twelve pages). It is reviewed and updated after each election on the advice of the Government Division of DPM&C, which provides assistance to agencies in interpreting the conventions during the caretaker period.

Increasingly, guidance documents are being presented as helping 'to avoid controversies about the role of the public service' during the caretaker period (DPM&C 2013). Passage of *the Public Service Act 1999* (Cth), sections 10 and 13 of which set out the 'Australian Public Service (APS) Values and Code of Conduct', has formalised public servants' obligations in this respect, incorporating in legislation explicit obligations regarding the behaviour of public servants. As part of its statutory responsibility to promote and uphold the Code, the Australian Public Service Commission (APSC) has developed educational resources to assist public servants, including the *Good Practice Guide: Supporting Ministers: Upholding the Values*. A short section of this guide deals briefly with issues that may arise during the caretaker period (APSC 2006, pp. 48–50).

State and territory jurisdictions have tended to follow the Commonwealth example, adopting the underlying principles and acknowledging the Commonwealth's lead in formalising, publishing and updating caretaker conventions. But different electoral timetables, local specificities and individual experience have meant the codified conventions are not consistent across all jurisdictions. The comparative analysis of different jurisdictional arrangements in Chapter 5 shows the nature and extent of some of these local variations.

In Queensland and South Australia, the caretaker conventions are spelt out in a *Cabinet Handbook*. In Tasmania, New South Wales and Victoria, they are issued as guidance documents by the respective Departments of Premier and Cabinet. In Western Australia, they are contained in a government memorandum to ministers issued by the Premier following the announcement of a general election. In the Australian Capital Territory and the Northern Territory, guidance documents are issued by the Chief Minister's Department.

Local government

Local governments in Australia are established under state legislation and have no constitutional recognition or status. State governments have broad powers in respect of local councils, including over their governance and the distribution of financial grants from the Commonwealth (Kane 2006). The legislative and operating framework for local councils takes the form of a *Local Government Act*, and Regulations established under that Act.

Until recently, local government was distinct from other tiers of Australian government in that no formal guidance was provided about the conduct of incumbents during election periods. The Victorian government first introduced 'caretaker arrangements' to cover the conduct of council elections, through amendments to the *Local Government Act 1989* (Vic) contained in the Local *Government (Democratic Reform) Act 2003* (Vic). This legislation introduced a range of electoral reforms, including caretaker provisions. These came into effect for the first time in elections for 25 Victorian local councils held in November 2004.

Since then, other jurisdictions have progressively amended their *Local Government Acts* to include the requirement for local councils to prepare and adopt a caretaker policy that governs the conduct of both councillors and staff in the period before the council election. The intent of the arrangements mirrors that of other jurisdictions, in that they are designed to avoid the use of public resources in a way that may unduly affect the election result and minimise councils making certain types of decisions that may limit the decision-making ability of the incoming council.

The introduction of fixed four-year terms for the majority of councils in Australia allows for an orderly management of decision-making leading up to the council election, and reduces the potential for major decisions needing to be made during an election period. As with all caretaker conventions, it is expected the regular business of council will continue. Restrictions are placed upon entering into major contracts, or appointing or terminating the chief executive officer during this time. The major focus is on not allowing the use of council resources for the advantage of candidates, particularly publications or public events which give a candidate a platform.

With the onus on individual councils developing their own caretaker policies, there has developed variability in caretaker requirements between councils. This can lead to neighbouring councils operating under different requirements. For example, the maximum amount of a contract that can be entered into during an election can vary from council to council. Councils are only directed to adopt 'minimum requirements' of prohibited activities during an election, so there remains scope to adjust their policies depending on local issues.

Significantly, caretaker arrangements for local government are legislated, and they have become matters of law, adjudicated by Ministers for Local Government, rather than matters purely of judgement, as characterises the situation in other levels of Australian government and internationally. The implications of these developments are yet to be tested, but if a council enters into a contract considered 'invalid' during an election period, the relevant Local Government Minister can void the contract and the council can be sued for compensation. The implication of the legislation of caretaker requirements for local government may indeed not yet be fully appreciated, but this represents a significant departure from practice in other Westminster-style political systems.

New Zealand

The development of the caretaker conventions in New Zealand has followed a similar trajectory to that of Australia. It is broadly agreed that New Zealand's arrangements have been shaped by three important experiences:

- the 1984 constitutional crisis
- the 'hung parliament' following the 1993 general election
- the adoption in 1996 of the mixed member proportional (MMP) electoral system.

The 1984 constitutional crisis

The July 1984 general election delivered a landslide victory to Labour, but it was expected to be around ten days before the return of the writs. Controversy arose, however, when outgoing National Party Prime Minister Sir Robert Muldoon refused to act on advice from the New Zealand Reserve Bank that the dollar should be devalued because of a run on the nation's foreign currency reserves.[4] The situation was exacerbated by the market's expectation that Labour would devalue the currency by between 15 and 20 per cent. After the election, as a currency crisis loomed, the defeated Muldoon refused to meet with officials over the weekend, despite their concerns that opening of the foreign exchange markets would trigger a financial crisis. Incoming Prime Minister David Lange supported devaluation and suggested that 'Muldoon should either implement the incoming Government's instructions or resign and let another member of the National Cabinet take over as caretaker Prime Minister for a week until Labour took office' (Gustafson 2000, p. 392). After much wrangling, Muldoon relented under pressure from his Cabinet colleagues,[5] but the situation raised questions about the authority and responsibilities of a defeated government during the period leading up to its formal replacement by an incoming administration.

The experience was a catalyst for more explicit guidance about the actions of outgoing governments during the caretaker period. Recommendations of a 1986 Officials Committee on Constitutional Reform were accepted by both parties. Boston et al. (1998, p. 636) note that 'the wording adopted by the Officials Committee corresponded closely to that employed at the time of the 1984 crisis by the outgoing Attorney-General, Jim McLay, in a press statement'.

---

4   In his biography of Muldoon, Barry Gustafson (2000, pp. 384–96) explains Muldoon's rationale for rejecting this advice. He had been in dispute with the Secretary to the Treasury and the Reserve Bank Governor over the matter for several months. Muldoon suspected that they were using the opportunity provided by the pre-election run on the New Zealand currency to re-prosecute advice he had previously rejected.

5   Who were prepared to advise the Governor-General that Muldoon no longer enjoyed their confidence and should hand over to his deputy.

Although formalised by its subsequent incorporation into *The Cabinet Manual*, the convention had been operative in that it was accepted by both the Labour and National Parties from the time of McLay's statement.

The initially hung parliament that followed the 1993 general election

In contrast to the situation in 1984, the outcome of the 1993 election was initially unclear. To address uncertainty over the conduct of business in the period until the new government could be determined, the Cabinet Office issued a circular outlining criteria for Cabinet and ministerial decision-making. It suggested that caretaker governments should refrain from significant decisions and outlined interim procedures to be followed in the event that urgent decisions were required — specifically, that these should be taken only after consultation with Opposition party leaders. As matters transpired, within a fortnight the National Party had achieved a clear (if slim) majority, leaving the proposed arrangements untested, notwithstanding their having bipartisan support. The criteria were subsequently incorporated into *The Cabinet Manual* in 1996 (Boston et al. 1998, p. 637).

The adoption of a mixed member proportional (MMP) electoral system from 1996

The adoption of a mixed member proportional (MMP) electoral system has had a profound impact on New Zealand's caretaker arrangements. Boston et al. (1998, p. 637) note that this development 'supplied the necessary political incentive for a more careful formulation of the conventions governing caretaker administrations'. The period between 1993 and 1996 was a time of transition, during which the constitutional implications of greater political uncertainty and longer caretaker periods were widely canvassed. The 1996 election — the first held under the new system — produced no clear result. The government remained in caretaker mode throughout the nine weeks it took to broker a coalition. Boston et al. (1998, pp. 68–73) describe the challenges created for the ongoing business of government in New Zealand by the unexpectedly lengthy caretaker period.

As a consequence of these experiences, and the expectation that longer transition times would become the norm in forming government in New Zealand, a new formulation was developed to give guidance to the period after the election but before the swearing in of the new government. The caretaker convention identifies 'two arms' of the convention, each of which has its own constitutional principles. The first arm applies when it is not clear who will form the next government, and the second applies when it is clear who will form government, but they have not yet taken office.

The caretaker convention also applies if the Government has clearly lost the confidence of the House. In that case, the convention guides the government's actions until a new administration takes office, following either negotiations between parties represented in the current Parliament, or a general election.

In New Zealand, the public and media attention falls on the transition period after the election, rather than the focus being on the conduct of politicians during the campaign, which characterises Australian elections. The complexities and uncertainties of New Zealand's electoral processes have necessitated development of highly prescribed caretaker arrangements and practices. *The Cabinet Manual* has been updated periodically in the 20 years since the introduction of MMP to incorporate the new understandings that have evolved through practice. Constitutional expert Elizabeth McLeay (1999, p. 12) notes:

> The treatment of caretaker government in successive editions nicely demonstrates how conventions evolve: through practical experience (good and bad); from observation of practices elsewhere; and through constitutional advice from the Crown Law Office, constitutional commentators, Prime Ministers and, of course, the Cabinet Office itself. Thus, many factors have influenced, and are continuing to influence, the formulation of rules on how caretaker governments should behave.

4. When Do the Conventions Apply?

The caretaker period begins at the time the Lower House (House of Representatives or Legislative Assembly) is dissolved and continues until the election result is clear or, if there is a change of government, until the new government takes office. The Queensland guidance notes that care should be exercised during the period between the announcement of the election and the dissolution of the Legislative Assembly, this being a particularly sensitive time requiring judgement and common sense. The New South Wales guidance — mindful of the fixed parliamentary terms in that state — specifies that caretaker conventions commence when the term of the Legislative Assembly expires. In Victoria and Tasmania, the period commences when the Legislative Assembly expires or is dissolved. In the Australian Capital Territory — which also has fixed four-year terms — the conventions apply from the beginning of the election period, which is 37 days before the polling day (ACT 2012, pp. 3–4).

Commencement of the conventions

Australian Commonwealth

Under the Australian Constitution, the House of Representatives continues for three years from the first meeting of the House and no longer, but may be dissolved earlier by the Governor-General (s. 28). The term of the current Parliament ends when the three-year term of the House of Representatives expires or is dissolved by the Governor-General on the advice of the government. There are two constitutional mechanisms by which this can occur:

- the dissolution of the House of Representatives (s. 5), or

- the simultaneous dissolution of both Houses — a double dissolution (s. 57).

A general election follows either the dissolution of the House or the expiration of its three-year term. The 'Governor-General in Council' (that is, acting on the advice of the Federal Executive Council) then issues a writ directing the Electoral Commissioner to conduct an election in accordance with prescribed procedures. The writ specifies the date on which the election will be held and the date for the return of the writ. It is deemed to have been issued at 6 p.m. on the date of issue.

Importantly, ministers sitting in the Senate, as members of the government, are bound by caretaker conventions for the period of the election until the outcome is known. This applies whether or not any Senate elections (periodical, general or territorial) are being held simultaneously with a general election for the House of Representatives.

The process that follows is outlined in Table 4.1.

Until 1925, the Australian Parliament was prorogued before the dissolution of the House of Representatives; this practice was discontinued between 1928 and 1993, but later reinstated on advice from legal experts (Odgers 2012, Ch. 19). Accordingly, in 1993 and 1996, Governors-General first prorogued Parliament by proclamation, issuing another proclamation on the same day to dissolve the Parliament. Since 1998, prorogation and dissolution have been combined in one proclamation.

An Executive Council meeting is usually held between the calling of the election and the issuing of the writs. This is a 'tidy-up' meeting that deals with last minute issues — such as the making of regulations under recently enacted legislation. This is seen as a legitimate housekeeping activity, but can be used cynically by governments — for example, as an opportunity to make last-minute appointments.

As noted, the timetable between the announcement of an election and the issuing of writs — that is, the period when caretaker conventions formally commence — can vary. Since 1940, the average gap has been nineteen days (Hughes and Costar 2006, p. 47). It has been argued that this reflected a 'convention' that some time should elapse between the announcement of the election and the issuing of the writs, since the latter coincides with the closure of the electoral rolls (Sawer 2006). Malcolm Fraser controversially altered this practice in 1983, when the writs were issued and the electoral rolls closed at 6 p.m. on the same day (4 February) as his surprise announcement of a double dissolution election for 5 March. Fraser was accused of excluding many thousands of citizens from exercising their right to vote and an action was mounted in the High Court, albeit unsuccessfully.

Table 4.1: Key dates in commencement of caretaker conventions — Australian Commonwealth[1]

Stage	Timeframe	Relevant Actor	Authority	Process
Prorogation of the Parliament/Dissolution of the House of Representatives		Governor-General on advice of Executive Council	Constitution, ss. 5, 28	Proclamation of prorogation and dissolution read by Official Secretary. Direction to Electoral Commissioner to conduct an election. These actions relate to the House of Representatives and periodical or general election of Senators.
Issue of writs (deemed to be 6pm)	Within 10 days of dissolution.	Governor-General.	Constitution s. 32; Commonwealth Electoral Act, ss. 151, 152	Caretaker conventions officially commence.
Close of electoral rolls	From 2007, 3 working days from date writ is issued. For new enrolments and re-enrolments from 8pm on date of writ. (Formerly 7 days after issue of writ.)	Electoral Commissioner	Commonwealth Electoral Act, ss. 102(4), 155	
Nominations close (at 12 noon)	Not less than 10 days nor more than 27 days after date of writ.		Commonwealth Electoral Act, ss. 156, 175	
Date of polling (a Saturday)	Not less than 23 days nor more than 31 days from date of nomination.		Commonwealth Electoral Act, ss. 157, 158	
	If election result is clear, caretaker conventions end. If not, continue until new government is sworn in.			
Return of writs	Not more than 100 days after issue.		Commonwealth Electoral Act, s. 159.	Electoral Commissioner certifies name of successful candidate in each division, returns writ to Governor-General. Forwarded by Official Secretary to Clerk of the House of Representatives.

1 Adapted from House of Representatives Practice, Chapter 3.

The Joint Select Committee on Electoral Reform (JSCER), established by the Hawke Labor government in 1983, considered the issue as part of a wide-ranging review of Australia's electoral system. It recommended a proclamation by the Governor-General to announce the election date a minimum of seven days before the issue of writs. Subsequent amendments to the *Commonwealth Electoral Act 1918* in 1983 inserted a stipulation that writs must be issued within ten days of the dissolution (s. 151(2)). The JSCER recommendation was incorporated as a separate provision (s. 155). This provision remained unchanged until the passage of the *Electoral and Referendum Amendment (Electoral Integrity and Other Measures) Act* (Cth) in 2006.[2] Section 151(2) remains unchanged by recent amendments.

Since the late 1980s, the time that has elapsed between the announcement of an election and the issuing of the writs has declined markedly. For elections held between 1990 and 2013, the average time that elapsed was around three days, with only one day between the 2013 election announcement and the issuing of the writs. However, the perception that a 'gap' exists between calling of the election and commencement of caretaker conventions remains strong (for example, see Charlton 2001). The bitterly fought 2001 election, held in the wake of the September 11 terrorist attacks, may have done much to fuel concerns about government actions in this period (see, for example, Marr and Wilkinson 2003).

Prime Minister John Howard visited the Governor-General on Friday, 5 October 2001, asking him to dissolve the House of Representatives for the 10 November election, but writs were not issued until midday on Monday, 8 October. During this intervening period, the United States launched air-strikes on Afghanistan in retaliation for the terrorist attacks on New York and Washington.[3]

At issue was whether the Prime Minister was obliged to consult the then Leader of the Opposition, Kim Beazley, about a decision to commit 1,000 Australian troops to the so-called 'War on Terror'. John Howard argued that he would 'observe the conventions', but that while he would inform Mr Beazley about developments, he would not make joint decisions. The Prime Minister noted:

> I'm quite ready to talk to Mr Beazley … but of course the decision-making still rests with me because I am still Prime Minister. You continue, of course, to govern and you certainly continue to take decisions within any existing established policy. (quoted in Gosch 2001)

---

2   Among other things, the Act amended section 155, reducing the seven-day period for closure of the electoral rolls to a period of three working days. For people who have not voted before, electoral rolls close at 8 p.m. the day the writs are issued. This has been a controversial change, aimed ostensibly at limiting the potential for fraudulent enrolments, but it may have the practical effect of excluding many young, first-time voters. For detailed analysis, see Hughes and Costar (2006).

3   Prime Minister Howard was advised of the US air strikes in a telephone call from Vice-President Dick Cheney early on the morning of 8 October 2001.

The government was also criticised for entering into an arrangement to process asylum seekers offshore in Papua New Guinea and Nauru (a policy that became known as the 'Pacific Solution'), just half an hour before caretaker conventions were due to commence at midday (Marr and Wilkinson 2003, pp. 178–9). This became the subject of contention during subsequent Senate estimates hearings, with government officials maintaining caretaker conventions had not been breached as (they argued) the agreements reached related to existing aid policy, and in any event were concluded before the conventions formally commenced (F&PA Committee 2002, pp. 192–7). Asked for advice on this matter, a senior DPM&C official noted that the situation was urgent (the fate of the asylum seekers could not await the election outcome), but that in the circumstances the Opposition should be advised of the decision and of the fact that any such decisions would bind any incoming government.

In 2004, controversy arose when a Senate Select Committee conducted a one-day hearing during the caretaker period. The committee had been established on 30 August 2004 to examine matters arising from public statements by a former ministerial staffer, Mike Scrafton, about conversations with the Prime Minister regarding the so-called 'Children Overboard' affair (which, perhaps ironically, had occurred during the 2001 election campaign). The Prime Minister had announced the election date on Sunday, 29 August, but the House was not dissolved, and the writs were not issued, until Tuesday, 31 August. The committee held a public hearing one day later, on 1 September. Questions were raised about the appropriateness of this action, given the politically contentious nature of the issues under consideration, and whether the prorogation of the Parliament meant the Senate should not be meeting. The issue of whether the Senate has a right to meet or exercise its powers after dissolution is highly contested, but the practice has been for the Senate not to meet between prorogation and before the opening of the new Parliament — although it has frequently authorised its committees to continue to do so.

Australian local government

Local government caretaker periods are specified in legislation. This period varies according to the particular state legislation, but normally the caretaker period begins on the day the nomination for candidates closes. For instance, in Victoria, the period is 32 days — the period from the last day of nominations until election day.

In Queensland, the election period is defined in section 25 (1) of the *Local Government Electoral Act 2011* (Qld): it 'starts on the day when public notice of the holding of the election is given' and 'ends at the conclusion of the election'.

For the Brisbane City Council, this period is as defined in section 3 of the *Electoral Act 1992* (Qld) as the period beginning on the day after an election writ is issued and ending at 6 p.m. on the polling day for the election.

New Zealand

New Zealand, with its unicameral parliament, has three-year fixed terms. The conventions apply from the dissolution of the House of Representatives. In the period immediately before a general election, although not bound by caretaker conventions, successive governments have chosen to restrict their actions to some extent at this time in recognition of the fact that an election — and therefore a potential change of government — is imminent. In practice, restraints have tended to be applied from approximately three months before the general election is due or, if the period between the announcement of the election and polling day is less than three months, from the announcement of the election (NZDPM&C 2008, pp. 76–7). The conclusion of the caretaker period can be difficult to predict in New Zealand. The MMP voting system means that there is a possibility of a lengthy period before the formation of a new government — as happened in 1996, for example, when the caretaker period lasted for nine weeks. The New Zealand caretaker conventions have a substantial section on guidance when it is not clear who will form the next government, in order to assist with decision-making during that interregnum.

Caretaker conventions after an election

The caretaker period concludes when the election result is known with either the confirmation of the continuation of the incumbent government, or the commissioning of a new government. Although this has mostly proved straightforward, the operation of caretaker conventions in the period after elections emerged as an issue in the late 1990s following close-run election results in New South Wales, Queensland and Victoria.

The 1995 election in Queensland brought an unexpectedly close result. The Labor Government under Wayne Goss was eventually returned with a one-seat majority in the Legislative Assembly about seventeen days after polling day. The Opposition then challenged the result in one seat, Mundingburra, in the Court of Disputed Returns. The judge ordered that a by-election be held in the seat on 3 February 1996. The by-election was won by the Liberal Party candidate and, with the support of independent Liz Cunningham, the Coalition under Rob Borbidge secured the confidence of the Legislative Assembly, and hence the ability to form government. Although the government had not been in caretaker mode because the House was not dissolved for a by-election, once the result was clear, and Cunningham had indicated her intention to support the Coalition, Opposition Leader Rob Borbidge, called on Premier Goss to 'observe the appropriate convention', and noted that 'the Goss Government should consider itself in a caretaker role only' (Reuters 1996).

In Victoria in 1999, the election result was unclear for almost a month after the polls closed. It took several weeks and a by-election following the death of a candidate on polling day for a minority government to be formed. The ALP under Steve Bracks secured the support of three independents to oust incumbent Premier Jeff Kennett. The situation posed a challenge for the Victorian public service, requiring it to understand and administer post-election caretaker arrangements until the new government could be sworn in (Davis et al. 2001, p. 18). As both parties courted the independents, political manoeuvring complicated the task, prompting the Department of the Premier and Cabinet to establish a reference group, supported by a secretariat, to support decision-making essential to keep the business of government running. Particularly problematic was the role of political advisers — both of incumbent and shadow ministers — who sought to act on behalf of their principals, creating difficulties for public service impartiality and neutrality.

The Victorian experience suggested a need for clear guidance on caretaker arrangements in the post-election period. Davis et al. (2001, pp. 25–6) propose some principles for the conduct of public administration in such circumstances, but these have gone largely untested.

The 2010 federal election saw, for the first time, the challenges of a long transition within the Commonwealth government. The media focus was firmly on the implications of a hung parliament and which party the independent cross-benchers would support to form government. To manage these unusual circumstances, the DPM&C quickly developed and distributed *Guidelines for Post-election Consultations with Independent Members* (DPM&C 2010). These guidelines advised that senior officials could hold discussions with independent members after agreement from the Prime Minister and after giving notice of the meeting to the Leader of the Opposition. This restricted public service advice to:

- matters relating to machinery of government and administration, including the administrative and technical practicalities and procedures involved in implementation of policies proposed by the government and Opposition parties

- information on the international, economic and budget outlook, including the costs of government and Opposition policies and their net impact on the Pre-Election Economic and Fiscal Outlook aggregate budget estimates, and

- factual information of the kind that an official might provide to a parliamentary committee.

During the seventeen days after the poll, the cross-bench MPs received briefings from eleven Departmental Secretaries (Reece 2012, p. 7). The post-election guidelines were not incorporated into the guidance for the 2013 election, prompting some to question whether the 2010 guidelines had been too narrowly framed, and thus represented a 'missed opportunity' for what over time proved not to be the aberration some regarded the 2010 result to be; rather, it was indicative of a more pluralistic and fragmented politics.

Four-year fixed terms

In Australia, introduction of fixed four-year terms for most states, territories and local councils has resulted in an orderly approach to the organisation of government business in the run-up to elections. For example, major contracts can be finalised and key appointments made without danger of these falling through because of the unexpected calling of an election. Parliamentary business can be completed and legislation presented for assent without the threat of Bills lapsing as the Parliament is dissolved. At present, only the Queensland and Commonwealth parliaments still adhere to three-year, non-fixed terms. It can be said that both jurisdictions suffer from the heightened uncertainty that this brings, and both have experienced controversies about the application of the caretaker conventions in recent years.

In Queensland, Premier Anna Bligh announced on 25 January 2012 than the election would be held on 24 March, and that she would seek the dissolution of Parliament on 19 February. Premier Bligh took the unusual step of announcing the election date early to allow some certainty for business and the electorate regarding the timetable. Though this situation is quite normal for jurisdictions with fixed terms, this announcement was portrayed in Queensland as a breach of the caretaker conventions. This view was echoed by Scott Prasser in an opinion piece in *The Australian* as being 'unprecedented in Australian politics' and having the air of 'political trickery' (Prasser 2012: 12). Yet it is quite clear that caretaker conventions take effect when the writs are issued and the Parliament is dissolved. After Anna Bligh's announcement, the Parliament continued to sit and the Labor government continued to be accountable to it.

The same controversy arose when Prime Minister Julia Gillard announced in January 2013 that the date for the next election was to be 14 September 2013. Critics forgot the connection between caretaker conventions and the sitting of Parliament. The conventions operate from the dissolution of the House of Representatives until the election result is clear, and are designed to begin when the executive government loses its accountability to Parliament. The majority of Australian jurisdictions now have fixed parliamentary terms, and are used to managing the months before the official beginning of the election period in a systematic manner. When the decision about when to call an election remains the political prerogative of the leader, as in Queensland and the Commonwealth, the pre-caretaker period tends to become involved as a weapon in political positioning.

The introduction of four-year fixed terms in most jurisdictions in Australia and New Zealand has taken the heat out many of the controversies that previously had attended their sudden application as an election was called. Bureaucracies are better prepared to enter the uncertainty of an election period, and can be confident the mechanisms are in place to carry them through to the establishment of the next government. This development has led to a more mature approach to managing the continuity of government business during election periods.

Conclusion

The issue of when caretaker conventions apply has been something of a concern in recent Commonwealth elections. Closer examination of arrangements governing commencement of the conventions suggests that the time period elapsing between the announcement of the election and the issuing of the writs to dissolve the House of Representatives has actually decreased in recent years. Our more adversarial politics and the emergence of the 'permanent campaign' mode of contemporary politics may account for persistent uncertainty over what governments might do, and when. Four-year fixed terms have addressed some of the 'gamesmanship' in which governments might engage immediately prior to the calling of an election. For jurisdictions like New Zealand, where election results can take some time to resolve, the issue of caretaker conventions in the post-election period has been more of an issue. Guidance documents have evolved to address the specific concerns of individual jurisdictions.

5. Caretaker Conventions: An Overview of Australian Jurisdictions

Each Australian jurisdiction has developed its own guidelines to support ministerial and departmental decision-making during the caretaker period. Guidances on the observance of caretaker conventions tend to be couched as general principles rather than strict, highly specific rules (Boston et al. 1998, p. 646) — although, when a well-publicised breach has occurred, the tendency has been to increase the detail in prescribing behaviour. Malone (2007, p. 5) notes 'the proper operation [of caretaker conventions] is dependent on the public servants who will make judgements on precisely what they mean and how they apply'. That is true, but they also depend to a significant extent on the attitude of the first minister and their receptiveness to advice.

In broad terms, caretaker conventions aim to ensure incoming governments are not bound by the last-minute decisions or actions of their predecessors, that the neutrality of the public service is preserved and that the substantial — and arguably increasing — advantages of incumbency are moderated. However, the government remains the government, and the ordinary business of public administration continues.

Within this accepted set of principles, each Australian jurisdiction has developed a guidance on the practice of the conventions locally. These guidance documents all acknowledge the over-arching principles and contain details about local application.

In this chapter, we draw on these guidance documents to present a detailed overview of caretaker arrangements. We look at the practices that have developed around specific issues and government activities. We use cases and examples to illustrate the complex and contested nature of caretaker conventions, and highlight areas of similarity and difference in practice.

Avoiding major policy decisions

All jurisdictions cite the taking of major policy decisions as a key area that falls under caretaker conventions. The adherence to three caretaker principles is involved in any decision concerning a major policy matter. These are: (1) not taking a decision for which the government (or minister) cannot formally be called to account in Parliament; (2) not binding an incoming government to a particular course of action; and (3) avoiding a decision that is a matter of contention between the government and the Opposition.

Nevertheless, the emphasis on what constitutes a policy decision is not consistent across all jurisdictions. A number of jurisdictions focus on the *taking of a policy decision* and others focus on the *implementation of a new policy*. For example, the Commonwealth, Tasmanian, Western Australian, New South Wales, ACT, South Australia and Northern Territory governments are concerned to ensure that major or significant policy decisions are not made during the caretaker period. 'Major or significant' is not specifically defined and remains a matter for judgement, though relevant considerations include assessing for policy and financial significance, and the likelihood the decision would be politically contentious.

The Queensland and Victorian governments' guidance documents state that the bureaucracy should avoid implementing major policy decisions during the caretaker period. This is a fine distinction that has important implications. The jurisdictions that are concerned about implementation of major policy decisions distinguish between prior and future policy intent. The implementation of major policy decisions does not infringe the conventions where decisions 'implemented before the expiry or dissolution of the Assembly are announced during the caretaker period' (Vic DPC 2010, p. 7). Most jurisdictions now distinguish between the 'making' of the policy commitment and its announcement. It is recognised that the conventions aren't contravened when commitments made before an election is called are then announced during the campaign.

Future policies are also exempt, with the majority of jurisdictions acknowledging that the 'conventions do not apply to promises on future policies that the party in government announces as part of its election campaign' (DPM&C 2013, p. 2) – although a number of jurisdictions warn that policies agreed to but not made public before the campaign should be announced ahead of the caretaker period if they are likely to be controversial (Tas DPC 2014, p. 3).

The sections of the guidance documents on the taking or implementing of major policy decisions acknowledge the reality of political incumbency, in that the government will be maximising its term in office by making decisions right up to the issuing of the writs for the election. Both sides will be making major policy commitments throughout the campaign, and these commitments will be the subject of extensive media analysis and debate. The claim that a decision was taken prior to the election is hard for an Opposition to challenge because of the confidentiality of Cabinet decisions. But this has not deterred Oppositions from making such claims in the heat of an election campaign.

Two examples illustrate this difficulty:

Signing Medicare funding agreements 1993

In 1993, the Keating Labor government announced that it had signed a five-year Medicare hospitals funding agreement with the Victorian and New South Wales governments just minutes before the Official Secretary read the proclamation to dissolve the House of Representatives for the general election. This action was criticised by the Opposition and the media because it would bind an incoming government to provide additional funding for those jurisdictions for a period of five years. The then Prime Minister was unrepentant in his defence of the decisions, arguing that the states' decisions to sign the agreement 'at one minute to midnight' showed they wanted the protection of Labor's health policy, even if Dr Hewson were elected (quoted in Kitney and Maley 1993). State ministers explained the decision in terms of their need for funding certainty: the Medicare agreement had been due to expire at the end of June 1993. In the event, the Coalition lost the election and the Keating Labor government provided $300 million in additional funding for public hospitals over the life of the agreement.

Deploying defence personnel to Iraq in 2004

In September 2004, more than two weeks into the caretaker period, the Howard government announced that it had despatched officers of the Special Air Service (SAS) to rescue two Australians feared kidnapped by insurgents in Iraq. The Opposition Labor Party claimed the government had breached the caretaker conventions by not consulting then Opposition Leader Mark Latham about the deployment. Then Defence Minister Robert Hill argued the decision was not binding on a future government and, moreover, that it had been 'taken in accordance with the contingency plan that had earlier been agreed by Cabinet' (AAP 2004). Prime Minister John Howard told reporters the decision to establish a hostage crisis team was taken by the National Security Committee of Cabinet before the election campaign. He said: 'the caretaker doctrine does not require a government to consult the Opposition in relation to the implementation of a decision taken before the caretaker mode commenced' (quoted in Seccombe and Allard 2004).

As these examples suggest, the environment for making judgements about the taking and implementation of policy decisions during the caretaker period is highly political, and subject to intense public scrutiny through the news media.

This has obvious implications for public sector officials and how they should act and manage the complexities which ensue. Managing the interpretation of what constitutes a major policy announcement is a matter for judgement.

Such judgements are not required in most matters of ongoing administration, which does and should continue during the caretaker period. The need for judgement arises when issues are contested between the opposing political parties and the matter is controversial. Public sector officials need to be aware of the requirement to act cautiously when there is no possibility of parliamentary oversight of executive decision-making (Wilson 1995). Judgement cannot be acquired at the calling of an election, but is built up over time and through experience. This is why only the most senior officials should be responsible for caretaker conventions, and why they often consult central agency experts when weighing up their decisions.

As an election approaches, senior departmental officers often take stock of factors relevant to the programs and decisions with which they have been dealing. They should be familiar with, for example, the level of bipartisan support for particular policies, whether there is significant community or stakeholder opposition and the potential for significant media attention. The closer the election, the more pressure there is for public sector officials to get things right — particularly if, for example, a recently announced government policy is unpopular with the Opposition. In all cases, it is imperative the bureaucracy behaves responsibly and dependably, rather than trying to second-guess who will win the election.

Moratorium on significant appointments

All jurisdictional guidance documents contain a section on avoiding significant appointments during the caretaker period, and there is a degree of unanimity on handling the issue between the different jurisdictions. The majority of jurisdictions state that the 'significance' of an appointment can be assessed through two considerations: the importance of the position and the likelihood that the appointment would be controversial. Many have codified the level of appointment with precision.

Tasmania and Western Australia offer a classification of what constitutes a 'significant appointment'. For Tasmania, it is the 'head or deputy head of an agency, head of a division or branch whose activities are deemed sensitive, members of statutory bodies and statutory office holders' (Tas DPC 2014, p. 4). Western Australia recommends no action be undertaken on senior officer positions classified PSA Level 8 and above (WADPC 2013, p. 6). New South Wales is not as prescriptive but identifies the elements that would qualify an appointment as 'significant'. They are 'seniority, importance and profile of the position, the duration of the appointment, the manner in which the appointment is to be made ... and also whether the proposed appointment is likely to be controversial' (NSWDPC 2011, p. 3).

Significant appointments should not be controversial because of the range of options available to manage the situation. The options are:

- appoint on a short-term or acting basis (to be confirmed at a later date)
- defer appointment until after the election
- consult the Opposition (although the Opposition may not accede).

Both Western Australia and Queensland also advise that if an employment contract is due to expire during the caretaker period, it is acceptable to issue a short-term contract for up to three months. Other options include an acting appointment or consulting with the Opposition (Vic DPC 2010, p. 7).

Jurisdictions have accepted that they should exercise constraint in making senior appointments during the caretaker period but, technically, caretaker conventions were developed to guide ministerial behaviour, not the behaviour of public servants. The limitation on appointments has evolved as a self-imposed constraint. The Commonwealth guidance mentions only that ministers should avoid making significant appointments and is silent on senior appointments within the public service.[1] The Commonwealth's concern is directed to appointment of members to statutory bodies and statutory office-holders. Other jurisdictions have expanded what would initially have been a concern about stacking boards in the dying days of a government to encompass all senior government appointments.

A level of prescription contained in a guidance document is usually an indication that it has been an area of controversy in the past. In Victoria in 1999, an appointment became an issue because, as noted in Chapter 3, the results of the election were not clear for nearly a month after polling day. The appointment of a new Auditor-General had been approved and announced before the election, but because the appointee was relocating from New Zealand, the formality of approval by the Governor-in-Council did not happen until he had taken up his position. The appointee had already signed a legally binding contract for the position. The Labor Opposition indicated that if it were to form government, it would support the appointment, but the Opposition did not support the signing of the instrument during the caretaker period (Davis et al. 2001, p. 18).

The 2013 federal election saw a controversy about an appointment of ABC journalist Barrie Cassidy to the Advisory Council for the Museum of Australian Democracy. The Opposition criticised the appointment during the election campaign because of the timing of the appointment and the perception Cassidy, who had served as press secretary to Prime Minister Bob Hawke, was a 'friend'

---

1   In fact, in the Commonwealth, ministers are explicitly prevented from intervening in public service appointments under section 19 of the Public Service Act 1999 (Cth).

of Labor (Packham 2013). The Advisory Council is an unpaid, honorary position so does not qualify as 'significant' in the usual sense; however, it did become controversial because the appointment was finalised on the day the writs were issued, although the then minister, Tony Burke, said the 'appointment had been in train for months and was approved by Cabinet' (Burke, quoted in Packham 2013). After meeting with new Attorney-General George Brandis after the election, Cassidy offered his resignation because he accepted the minister's view that he did not think it appropriate for those currently involved in the political process to sit on the board (ABC News 2013). In his own statement, Brandis blamed 'the questionable process of the former government' as his key concern (Brandis 2013).

This appointment demonstrates the arbitrary nature of what can become controversial during an election campaign. In itself, the appointment was not significant, but the high profile of the appointee made it controversial, as did the perceived timing of the appointment. However, Cassidy might have been an unknown victim of a flawed process, with the appointment having been in train for months and the lack of an earlier announcement explained by the then minister with the words, 'I thought it would have been announced by the department' (Burke, quoted in Kenny 2013).

Avoiding signing major contracts, undertakings and agreements

All guidance documents contain a section addressing the need for governments to avoid entering into major contracts or undertakings. The guidances reflect commercial realities by recognising the need for much of the work of government to continue during the caretaker period. Consideration is therefore given to the definition of the word 'major', with the most common definitions revolving around the monetary value of the contract, whether proceeding with it would entrench a 'policy, program or administrative structure', and whether the contract requires ministerial approval (Commonwealth, Tasmania, Victoria, Northern Territory). The Victorian guidance contains some additional material about allowing the entering into of contracts that are subsidiary to an existing 'head contract' during the caretaker period.

Most guidance documents acknowledge the difficulty of deferring contractual commitments for legal or commercial reasons, and suggest options if this is the case. These include:

- consultation with the Opposition
- consultation with the contractor to see whether the contract could be renegotiated

- the development of contracts that include a clause providing for termination in case an incoming government does not wish to proceed.

Jurisdictions with fixed parliamentary terms may find managing contractual arrangements less complex, since the regular election date is known in advance.

The management of contracts is routine administration for many departments, and often involves long lead-times. The guidance documents suggest that caution should be exercised in cases that fall under the definition of 'major', or that require ministerial approval.

Controversy arises when contracts are seen to breach caretaker conventions by giving electoral advantage to the incumbent government, or when they are interpreted as seeking to entrench a controversial policy. Such contention was avoided in Victoria in 1999, when the Minister for Health — who had been defeated at the election but who remained the minister pending the swearing in of the new government — delegated to the Secretary of his Department responsibility for finalising a contract that, if not executed within a specified time-frame, would attract significant penalties. This action was taken on the grounds that the Minister believed it was inappropriate to deal with it himself. The matter was resolved by officials in consultation with the Premier, the Leader of the Opposition, the Shadow Health Minister, political advisers and bureaucrats (Davis et al. 2001, pp. 18–19). The long delay in forming a new government in Victoria after the 1999 election was problematic for other types of contracts. Davis et al. (2001, p. 19) report that new procedures were required to allow urgent contracts to be finalised in the post-election caretaker period.

The responsibilities of government-owned corporations during the caretaker period are often complex. These entities are at arm's length from the core departments, but report to ministers, and hence are bound by the caretaker conventions. They are wise to exercise caution in the caretaker period, especially when their operations — or even their mere existence is controversial. As well, the corporations' obligations must be balanced against commercial considerations — such as, for example, where a delay would attract contract penalties or significantly disrupt a project that had been approved and already commenced.

During the 2013 federal election, the role of the National Broadband Network Company (NBN Co.) was in the spotlight. The two major political parties held different policy positions about how best to deliver high-speed broadband to Australian homes and businesses. Then Shadow Minister Malcolm Turnbull was highly critical of the company's former chief executive, Mike Quigley, and the NBN Co. board. When Quigley resigned in July 2013, the board commenced an executive search for his replacement. However, in August 2013, the company confirmed it would follow the caretaker conventions, suspending the search for its new CEO pending the outcome of the September poll. It undertook not to enter into new construction contracts, since that might limit a future government's options with respect to the NBN rollout, but it would continue business-as-usual activities, including construction of the network under existing contracts (Taylor 2013).

Intergovernmental negotiations and official visits

Intergovernmental negotiations

The focus of jurisdictional advice on intergovernmental negotiations centres on attendance at ministerial councils and forums, where it could be expected (by other governments) that someone from the relevant jurisdiction would be involved. The Commonwealth and Tasmania are silent on such negotiations, but other jurisdictions are in close agreement that, if possible, the government should seek to defer negotiations. If the interests of the state need to be represented at the Council of Australian Governments (COAG) or a ministerial council, it is accepted practice for a senior official to attend with observer status and with a limited role of supplying factual information on past positions. It is quite clear that no commitment or agreement should be entered into that would commit an incoming government.

The option of seeking Opposition agreement to a negotiating position is also canvassed by some jurisdictions. The lead time for major Commonwealth–state negotiations is quite considerable, and with the majority of jurisdictions on fixed terms, this is an area that has not been open to major breaches. The frequent number of elections in Australia means that senior officials are well versed in handling these protocols. The long lead times around negotiated agreements and the annual nature of most ministerial council meetings have left this area relatively free of controversy. However, some negotiations can leak into the caretaker period, and we consider these and other pressures on the observance of caretaker conventions in Chapter 7.

Official visits

Official visits of dignitaries are not covered by guidance documents in all jurisdictions. New South Wales, Western Australia and the Australian Capital Territory are silent on this issue. The other jurisdictions have a high level of unanimity regarding how visits from dignitaries should be handled.

The common advice is to defer the visit if possible, with either the Prime Minister or relevant Premier taking the decision. Dignitaries who have scheduled a visit should be advised of the calling of the election and the reduced availability of ministers to meet them. The Commonwealth, with its responsibility for foreign affairs, recommends the government either seeks to defer negotiations or adopt observer status (DPM&C 2013, p. 3).

Dealing with requests from ministerial offices

Requests from ministerial offices during an election campaign can be a source of conflict and uncertainty between the government and the bureaucracy. It is often an area where the government tries to push the advantages of incumbency and exert pressure on what had been a responsive bureaucracy. The elements of advice from the guidance documents are consistent in how to deal with requests from ministerial offices. During the caretaker period, departments are restricted to giving factual advice — not policy advice — to ministerial offices. It is acknowledged that ministers can determine the use to which the material can be put, though it is obviously inappropriate for officials to assist with adding this material to party political material. The majority of jurisdictions have a caveat on the supply of information based on the Commonwealth guidance, which suggests it is appropriate to decline a request if it requires 'the use of significant resources and was clearly for use in an election campaign' (DPM&C 2013, p. 7).

The majority of guidances remind officers to avoid any perception of partisanship in their dealings with ministerial offices, and the sensitivity of this interaction is acknowledged by advising that any concerns should be referred to the department's CEO or to the CEO of the central agency. It is accepted that the level of judgement required with regard to some requests should not be the responsibility of a junior officer. The South Australian guidance, for example, recommends all communication with a ministerial office pass through the CEO's office (SADPC 2013, p. 8). This would enable agencies to operate at arm's length from political activity while the ongoing business of government continues.

Once again, it is stressed that the day-to-day business of government continues. The Commonwealth, Victorian and Tasmanian guidances all acknowledge that, given the potential for urgent domestic or international issues to arise, advice should be provided to protect Australia's or the state's interests. This is particularly relevant in the areas of federal responsibility for defence and national security, where international crises and circumstances mean Australia could be in a position of needing to agree on a new policy during a caretaker period.

Restrictions on advertising and information campaigns

The handling of government advertising and information campaigns reveals divergent practice among Australian jurisdictions, and is an area that has seen tightening up of procedures in recent years. All jurisdictions agree on the need to be able to continue to disseminate material in the public interest and to stop communications that represent a political interest. Campaigns cited as addressing the public interest include defence recruitment, health promotion, road safety or material of an operational nature. There is general agreement that material can be classified as political if it highlights government achievements and policies, features the minister or is a matter of contention between parties. Decisions on advertising and information campaigns need urgent attention at the beginning of an election campaign.

Jurisdictions have developed different mechanisms to handle decision-making on the continuation of advertising and marketing campaigns. The Commonwealth[2] and Western Australian governments identify the head of a department as the responsible officer to make the recommendation on what campaigns should be discontinued. Queensland and Tasmania leave the decision at the political level, with the Premier deciding on which campaigns to curtail. The ACT introduced legislation in 2009 to appoint an independent reviewer, who is not a public servant, to report the Legislative Assembly on proposed campaigns. For South Australia and the Northern Territory, individual agencies review all public information campaigns and decide which to defer. Victoria has a mixed model, in which agencies review all campaigns scheduled to take place during the caretaker period, with any that promote government policies being sent to ministers for review. New South Wales has addressed the concerns about governments ramping up advertising before the caretaker period by introducing a 'quarantine period' for two months prior to the state election. The *Government Advertising Act 2011* (NSW) legislates to prohibit any party political material in government advertising, and has a provision for a governing political party to pay back the costs of any campaign that breaches the legislation (NSW Government 2012, p. 4).

This mixture of approaches demonstrates the dual nature of caretaker conventions. Is it a guide for ministerial behaviour or a guide for departments to manage within the intense atmosphere of an election campaign? The divide is explicit in the handling of advertising campaigns, where some departments take back the decision-making as a check on the power of incumbency while

---

2   In the Commonwealth, the Departments of Finance and Deregulation and Prime Minister and Cabinet undertake the review.

others leave the management of the decision to the head of the government, the Premier. The Commonwealth guidance makes it explicit that bipartisan agreement should be sought for campaigns that are to continue.

Government advertising has proved highly contentious in recent years, and has been described as 'the single most significant benefit of incumbency' (Young 2005). These issues were canvassed in a Joint Standing Committee on Electoral Matters inquiry into the conduct of the 2004 election. In her submission, Melbourne University academic Sally Young identified a number of instances where the government's use of advertising might have been questionable. These included what Young (2005, p. 3) describes as an extensive 'warm-up' period in the lead-up to the election campaign, during which there was a very large increase in government spending on advertising. Although she notes it is not unusual to see 'spikes' in government advertising expenditure immediately prior to an election, 'what was unusual in 2004 was the extent of pre-election spending and the sheer variety of government ads that were run. The federal government spent somewhere between $32 and $40 million between May and June alone.'

'Even more startling,' according to Young (2005, p. 3), 'was the government's reluctance to forgo government advertising even during the election campaign.' The 'Help Protect Australia against Terrorism' campaign ran extensively on TV, radio and in newspapers during the election period. Under caretaker conventions, this campaign had to be approved by Labor. Media reports suggest that the government 'had Labor over a barrel' with the anti-terrorism campaign. If it refused, it could be 'accused of preventing the community from being warned about the dangers of terrorism' (*Canberra Times* 2004). Labor agreed to the ads continuing on terms negotiated with the government, including the stipulation that the ads must specify they were authorised by the Australian Federal Police (AFP).

By Boat, No Visa campaign

These issues were replayed in the 2013 federal election campaign with the issue of government advertising once again on the front page. The Rudd government decided to continue the $30 million *By Boat, No Visa* campaign during the election. The ads were run in mainstream media, including television, radio and newspapers, and were aimed at deterring asylum seekers from travelling to Australia by boat. In line with the *Guidance on Caretaker Conventions*, all advertising campaigns were reviewed at the beginning of the caretaker period by the Departments of Finance and Deregulation and the Prime Minister and Cabinet. Bipartisan agreement was then sought for campaigns that were to continue. In the case of the *By Boat, No Visa* campaign, Opposition Leader Tony Abbott wrote to Prime Minister Rudd advising that the Opposition did not support the continuation of these ads in Australia (Abbott 2013a).[3]

When the government decided to continue airing the advertisements, the Opposition Leader then followed up with a letter to the Secretary of the Department of the Prime Minister and Cabinet, Dr Ian Watt, asking him to enforce the convention. The Secretary replied:

> responsibility for observing the conventions ultimately rests with decision makers, be they agency heads or, in the cases where they are involved, with Ministers and/or the Prime minister. Decision makers, including Ministers, are not prevented from making decisions, as the conventions are not legally binding. The Department does not have the power to enforce the observance of the conventions. (Watt 2013c)

In defending this decision, Immigration Minister Tony Burke said the caretaker conventions provided for consultation and that had occurred (Ross 2013). The independent Auditor-General, Ian McPhee, was also involved in the controversy when a complaint about the continuation of the ads was made to him. His response was 'the caretaker conventions give the government latitude when it comes to advertising campaigns, and noted in any case the conventions were not legally binding' (Morozow 2013).

Following the election of the Liberal coalition government, the Secretary of the Department of Finance, David Tune was asked about the continuation of the advertising at the Senate Estimates hearings. He described his involvement:

> The issue was on this occasion we were in the caretaker period and there are conventions around actions by public servants in that period of time, which I take seriously as a secretary and my department takes seriously. There was a contrary view. As a result of that the direction occurred (Senate Estimate Hearing 2014:43).

The Secretary went on to say he could not recall another instance where a senior official was directed by a Minister to continue on an advertising campaign during an election.

This controversy exemplifies the circular arguments that can revolve around caretaker controversies. The department makes a recommendation; the government can choose to ignore the recommendation; and the Opposition tries in vain to find an avenue to have the decision overturned. As Ian Watt pointed

---

3   In his 6 August 2013 letter to Prime Minister Rudd, Tony Abbott agreed to the continuation of the 'offshore' component of the advertising campaign, but found the 'onshore' component was 'being used for partisan political purposes within Australia' (Abbott 2013b).

out in his letter to Tony Abbott, the respective Secretaries were directed by their ministers to continue the campaign. He said 'both Secretaries have complied with the directions, as they are required to under the *Public Service Act*' (Watt 2013c). Watt's letter makes clear the basis on which the advertising campaign would continue — at the lawful direction of ministers, which by law and convention, officials are bound to follow. His response can be read as an effort to safeguard public service neutrality amidst a bitter and rapidly escalating partisan battle. Both the 2004 and 2013 advertising controversies show that both sides of Parliament will weather the controversy on continuing advertising campaigns because they see the political value of the campaign as outweighing the damage from the objections of the Opposition.

The management of government advertising during an election campaign is further complicated by being covered by electoral legislation. The basis of the Commonwealth and state Acts revolves around the need for authorisation of any material that may affect voting patterns, with the concern of attracting a penalty if the legislation is breached.

There is less concern about managing printed material during a campaign. The guidelines around printed material generally leave the decision to the discretion of the department, based on the previous criteria — does the material promote the policies of the government, contain photos of ministers or focus on government achievements? The key point in the guidance documents is to avoid active distribution of material that could be seen to promote party political content. The passive distribution of material through responding to requests or making it available in public places is considered acceptable.

Use of internet and electronic communications

Concern about misuse of the internet and electronic communications is a fairly recent addition to many guidance documents, and the instructions given have become increasingly detailed. For the majority of jurisdictions, the starting point is that agencies are responsible for ensuring that government resources are not used to support any political party. To do this, the majority of guidances recommend agencies review their websites at the beginning of the caretaker period. They can then determine whether any material needs to be removed from agency websites, as well as any ministerial websites supported and maintained by that agency. Ministerial statements that criticise the Opposition are cited as an example of material that should be removed. The advent of social media and increased interactivity of government websites has meant the addition of new directions to manage these functions. Most jurisdictions recommend agencies moderate previously unmoderated discussion forums and blogs, as well as posting a message explaining the restrictions of the caretaker period and advising that political material posted will be removed.

The guidances make a distinction between what can be added to *agency* websites and *ministerial* websites during the campaign. For example, it is generally agreed that agencies should only add portfolio-related announcements, factual material and material on existing policies and programs. For ministerial websites maintained by departments, it is agreed that only purely factual material should be added, and no material about future policies, how-to-vote material, political speeches and media releases that criticise the Opposition. The wisdom of adding exit or entry messages, particularly to ministerial websites that link to party political sites, is canvassed. The use of these messages draws a line between what is a funded government website and what is a link outside of the government domain. The Commonwealth's *Guidance on Caretaker Conventions* is supplemented in this area by the Australian Government Information Management Office Guidance on Departmental and Ministerial Websites (AGIMO 2013).

Government websites

The use of government websites provoked controversy during the 2004 federal election campaign. In September 2004, Opposition Finance Spokesman Bob McMullan wrote to then Secretary of Defence Ric Smith, alleging that then Minister Robert Hill had breached the caretaker conventions by posting four election-related announcements on a website maintained by the Department of Defence after the campaign had commenced (Kerin 2004). Of particular concern to Labor was the announcement of a new Defence headquarters at Bungendore, in the Coalition-held marginal seat of Eden-Monaro. McMullan argued that since it related to future policies and election commitments, the announcement should have been posted on the Liberal Party website.

In his letter of response to the shadow minister, the Secretary explained that Defence had closely followed the guidance document issued by the Department of the Prime Minister and Cabinet. He noted the website in question was not a departmental website, but one defined in the conventions as an agency-maintained 'ministerial website'. In accordance with the conventions, Defence put a notice on the website stating that no political or election-related material would be available on the website. The same notice appeared as a 'pop-up message' to advise visitors when they were leaving the website. Smith's letter also noted that the conventions are not infringed when decisions taken prior to the commencement of the caretaker period are announced during an election campaign. He reiterated his appreciation of the sensitivity of matters raised by the Opposition, but stated his belief that Defence was and had been discharging its duties diligently and professionally. However, he advised the shadow minister that, in order to 'minimise the risk of controversy', henceforth 'all of the media materials generated by our ministers and parliamentary secretary since 31 August [commencement of the caretaker period], and all future media materials, will now be posted by ministerial staff to the website of the Liberal Party of Australia' (Department of Defence 2004).

This example underscores the sensitivity of issues raised during the caretaker period, and the need for careful judgement when weighing questions of whether an incumbent government is advantaged through the support services available to ministers in the normal course of administration. It also demonstrates the contested interpretation of the conventions, particularly in areas of new and emerging practice. Notwithstanding the Secretary's confidence that Defence had adhered to the conventions, he initiated a change in the procedure followed — a concession, perhaps, that the principle of avoiding APS involvement in election activities should be the dominant consideration in this instance. As expected, more detailed advice on websites and electronic communications is included in the DPM&C caretaker conventions guidance issued in August 2007. The 2013 Guidance states that 'as a general rule during the caretaker period, ministerial media releases and alerts should be placed on the website of the relevant political party' (DPM&C 2013, p. 5). New advice about interactive and funded websites (DPM&C 2013, p. 5) illustrates the impact of emerging issues and technologies on the evolution of caretaker practices.

As well as detailed guidance about the management of agency and ministerial websites, the majority of jurisdictions caution that departmental email and bulletin boards should not be used to publish political material.

The Queensland guidance document is silent on the management of the internet and electronic communications during an election campaign. However, in Queensland, advice on the management of ministerial websites is provided in a letter from the Director-General of the Department of the Premier and Cabinet to each department head when caretaker conventions commence. It mirrors the advice provided in other jurisdictions. South Australia puts the obligation on ministers to ensure that political material is not present on publicly funded websites.

The Northern Territory takes a slightly different approach, consistent with the approach to advertising material. It recommends that all agency websites carry an authorisation identifying the senior officer who is responsible for comment on the website. It also recommends the use of entry and exit statements so users are clear about when they are no longer within a government site (NTDCM 2012, p. 16).

Social media

The growth of digital communications, and the use of social media tools such as Facebook, LinkedIn and Twitter to deliver public information and services, have necessitated new advice and guidance about how these activities should be managed during the caretaker period. The Commonwealth guidance recommends that agencies adopt approaches similar to those that apply to ministerial websites. It notes that AGIMO issues additional technical guidance about the use of interactive online engagement tools for federal employees. In 2013, the Australian Government Chief Technology Officer used his blog to issue advice about the application of caretaker conventions to government websites and via social media (Sheridan 2013). He emphasised the need to moderate comments or communications that could be viewed as contentious, or as conferring advantage on the incumbent government; and to carefully monitor online promotional or awareness-raising activities. He referred officials seeking further information to related guidance from the Australian Public Service Commission (APSC 2012).

The need for detailed guidance on the use of electronic communications during an election campaign is a useful illustration of the dynamic nature of caretaker conventions, and their flexibility in adapting to changing imperatives — in this case, rapid developments in technology.

Using the public service for policy costings

There is no set approach across jurisdictions to the issue of costing election policy commitments. Queensland, South Australia and the Northern Territory are silent on the issue. The Commonwealth has the most detailed guidance on policy costings. The guidance is given statutory sanction in the *Charter of Budget Honesty Act 1998* (Cth).[4] This Act outlines the process for the costing of election commitments by both the government and the Opposition. The Act states the Prime Minister may request the secretaries of the Departments of Treasury and/or Finance to prepare costings of publicly announced government policies. Requests from the Leader of the Opposition are given to the Prime Minister, who may agree to refer them to the responsible Secretaries. The onus is then on the responsible Secretary to release the policy costings before polling day.

To further complicate this process, the federal Parliament established the Parliamentary Budget Office (PBO) in 2012. It was established as an independent body to provide to the Parliament an independent analysis of forward estimates

---

4   For a detailed assessment of the Charter of Budget Honesty's genesis and early performance, see Wanna et al. (2000, pp. 245–58). For more recent, critical appraisals, see McMullan (2007) and Wanna (2006).

and the financial implications of policy proposals. Within the caretaker period, it can prepare election policy costings for either a parliamentary party or an Independent (DFD 2012).

Both New South Wales and Tasmania have legislated a Charter of Budget Honesty which allows for both the Premier and the Leader of the Opposition to request costings of publicly announced policies. Victoria allows the Department of the Treasury and Finance, in conjunction with the relevant agency, to cost government and non-government policies as long as the assumptions for the costings are identified and agencies are not required to undertake extensive policy research. Requests are made through the Premier, and a political party may only request costings of its own policies. In Western Australia, the *Financial Responsibility Act 2000* (WA) ensures the Treasurer releases a financial projections statement within ten days of the dissolution of the Legislative Assembly. Major political parties can then request costings of election commitments directly from the Under Treasurer — a different approach from other jurisdictions, which maintain a political control over requests through the Premier. Like Western Australia, the Australian Capital Territory allows for costings to be directed to the Treasury Directorate, and to be released publicly by the Director-General prior to the polling day.

Use of agency premises

The majority of jurisdictions accept the 'appropriate' use of government premises for media conferences and functions during an election campaign. The formula for determining 'appropriateness' is that if agency resources are involved, it is appropriate for the Opposition spokesperson, member or candidate to also be invited. Public servants should be even-handed in giving assistance to both government and Opposition. This general approach is used by the Commonwealth, Victorian, South Australian, Northern Territory, Tasmanian and ACT governments. All agree it is not appropriate for public servants to provide logistical support for political functions.

This use of agency premises is less developed than some other areas of concern within caretaker conventions. For example, no guidance is given on who is to arbitrate on this issue — it appears to be left to the discretion of local managers. In Western Australia, if Members of Parliament or candidates wish to visit a government facility, the CEO must be notified and they are to be accompanied by a representative during the visit. The New South Wales guidance states Members of Parliament wanting to visit agency premises have to seek the permission of the minister, except when the premises are in their own electorate.

Queensland is silent on the issue within its guidance documents, but expects that, during an election campaign, agencies will continue to use protocols that already exist to manage visits to government facilities.

This is an issue which can have local application in a way that many of the other conventions do not, as local officers are required to take decisions about political figures with whom they have an ongoing working relationship. Visiting departmental premises also became politicised. During the last federal election the Queensland Education Minister, John-Paul Langbroek, banned federal Education Minister Peter Garrett from visiting two state schools. The Queensland minister said 'schools are being used as political stages' and 'we don't think this is good for either students or staff' (Bourke 2013).

Pre-election consultation with the Opposition

Most jurisdictions have quite detailed and prescriptive advice on how the public sector should handle consultations with the Opposition. The focus of the advice is on the government restraining and limiting the bureaucracy in its dealing with non-government parties. This differs from the general focus of the guidance documents, which is based on giving the bureaucracy support and advice in constraining the behaviour of the incumbent party.

A very similar process is outlined in each guidance document. The accepted procedure is for the Opposition spokesperson to make application to the minister, who then forwards it either to the Prime Minister or Premier for consideration. In the Commonwealth, ministers decide whether to agree or not, and then advise the Prime Minister of the request and the decision. Guidance documents stress that the approach must come from the non-government parties, not officials. The scope of the meeting is limited to machinery of government, administrative and technical issues: it is stressed that officials are not authorised to discuss government policy or give opinions. The discussions are confidential, but ministers are entitled to inquire whether the meeting stayed within the agreed purposes. It is worth noting that the Commonwealth, Victorian and Queensland governments apply a different commencement time to the process of consultation with the Opposition than the application of the more general caretaker conventions. Consultation can commence, in the case of the Commonwealth and Victoria, three months prior to the expiry of the House of Representatives (Commonwealth) and two months in Queensland, or the date the election is announced — whichever comes first.

There are some differences between jurisdictions. For example, in Queensland an official from the Department of the Premier and Cabinet sits in on the meeting with the departmental CEO. Queensland is also quite specific that no special material should be prepared, and that only existing material such as annual reports or program statements should be made available. Western Australia has slightly reversed the process, in that the Opposition approaches the minister, who then refers the matter to the CEO, who is responsible for advising the minister when discussions have taken place: the minister then advises the Premier.

The Commonwealth guidance notes that consultation guidelines are different from caretaker conventions. As noted, the guidelines were first tabled in the House of Representatives in December 1976. These initial guidelines allowed direct approaches to departments by Opposition spokespeople. They were subsequently amended. The new guidelines were presented to the Senate on 5 June 1987. Consultation with the Opposition remains a contentious issue, with some senior public servants concerned that shadow ministers may see briefings as opportunities to score points on their opponents through their portfolio agencies.

Post-election consultation

The caretaker period ends when the election result is clear, or if there is a change of government, until the new government is appointed. Most elections deliver clear results, but occasionally – as in New South Wales in 1991, Queensland in 1998, Victoria in 1999, the Commonwealth and Tasmania in 2010, and South Australia in 2014, it took some time for the final result to be determined and for political parties to negotiate the support necessary to form government.

Some argue there is an increasing trend to minority governments (see, for example, Reece 2012), and that this will necessitate greater attention to caretaker conventions in the post-election period, as is routine in jurisdictions like New Zealand (see Chapter 6). For the public service, uncertainty in the aftermath of an election creates a range of practical problems. Who is eligible to receive advice and briefing from departments? How should agencies manage the preparation of incoming government briefs when the composition of the government and the timing of the swearing in of a new government are unclear?

Non-finalised legislation

Guidance on what happens with non-finalised legislation appears rather vague and variable. The formulation used by the Commonwealth, New South Wales and Victoria is that if Bills have passed through both Houses, they should be assented to by the Governor-General or Governor before the dissolution of the

Lower House. In respect of Bills passed by both Houses, but still awaiting Royal Assent after the dissolution, the Commonwealth Office of Parliamentary Counsel (OPC) notes that 'it would be improper for such Bills not to receive assent' (OPC). The Commonwealth guidance acknowledges the constitutional uncertainty about the validity of Acts that receive assent in the period between dissolution and the opening of the new Parliament. To avoid such controversies, the OPC endeavours to ensure that all such Bills are assented to prior to dissolution of the House.

Queensland is quite specific that Bills introduced but not passed lapse, as do Bills awaiting Royal Assent. South Australia and Western Australia have a slightly different practice in that all Bills that have not passed through both Houses automatically lapse when the Lower House is dissolved. South Australia makes provision for legislation passed and assented to before the election to be proclaimed during the caretaker period. In Western Australia, there is provision for Bills to be given assent during the caretaker period, notwithstanding the dissolution of the Legislative Assembly. Western Australia allows for Bills to be proclaimed when they come into operation during the caretaker period. The Tasmanian formula is that Bills passed by both Houses should be assented to by the Governor, but may lawfully receive assent later. Tasmania also has provision for legislation to be 'proclaimed' during the caretaker period, but with the caveat that the decision to make the proclamation should not be made once the caretaker period has begun. Proclamations that fall within this period (made from earlier decisions) will still have effect.

The approaches of the Australian Capital Territory and the Northern Territory are slightly different. The ACT allows for a minister to approve by gazettal the commencement of legislation that has been passed in the Legislative Assembly. In the Northern Territory, Bills that have been introduced to the Legislative Assembly but not passed automatically lapse, although every effort should be made before prorogation to gain assent from the Administrator to those Bills already passed. There is a capacity, based on the advice of the Clerk of the Legislative Assembly, for a proposed law to be presented to the Administrator for consent during the caretaker period.

There is general agreement among all jurisdictions on the handling of subordinate legislation. Where there is no infringement of the caretaker conventions, it is considered acceptable for subordinate legislation to be approved by the Governor-in-Council, or equivalent, during the caretaker period. So, for instance, a Governor may approve minor amendments to traffic regulations if they are forwarded by the Transport Department during the caretaker period.

Meetings of Executive Council

All jurisdictions identify some capacity for the Executive Council to meet during the caretaker period, but with different levels of advice on whether the meeting should be routine or exceptional. For example, the Commonwealth, Victoria, New South Wales, Tasmania and Western Australia all make provision for limited and infrequent meetings to deal with routine business such as regulations and ordinances. Queensland does not hold ordinary meetings of the Executive Council during the caretaker period, but a special sitting can be held with the consent of the Governor and the Premier. Each jurisdiction offers the caveat that the business considered should not infringe the caretaker provisions concerning the taking of major decisions or binding an incoming government. To decrease the necessity for the Executive Council to meet during the caretaker period, most jurisdictions make provision for a 'tidy-up' meeting before commencement to approve new regulations.

In South Australia, it is accepted practice for the Executive Council to operate after the dissolution of the House of Assembly. The guidance cites the principle of the separation of powers to support that view. In the Northern Territory, the advice suggests that the Executive Council should cease, although provision is made to convene in exceptional circumstances. Although there is differing practice across jurisdictions, the general consensus is that there is a need to provide for the management of non-controversial routine business of government.

Meetings of Cabinet

The majority of jurisdictions are either silent on the meeting of Cabinet during the caretaker period, or acknowledge that it would not meet. If Cabinet did need to meet, items considered would be consistent with the caretaker conventions. The exception is South Australia, which states that during the caretaker period the normal business of executive government continues because of the separation of powers between the Parliament and the Executive. Cabinet can continue to meet for routine matters, but not major undertakings, initiatives or appointments. This is a different interpretation from other jurisdictions, which base their approach on the convention of responsible government holding that, with the dissolution of the House, the executive cannot be held responsible for its decisions in the normal manner.

A crisis situation might necessitate a Cabinet meeting during the caretaker period. This was the case in 1914 with the outbreak of the First World War during a Commonwealth election campaign (see Weller 2007, pp. 30–2).

Cabinet and other documents

The management of Cabinet documents during an election campaign falls under another set of conventions guiding the working of Cabinet. The convention is that Cabinet documents and decisions are confidential to the government that created the documents, and are not made available to successive governments. All jurisdictions cite this convention and adhere to the same process. Each department is responsible for retrieving and securing its Cabinet documents ready for return to the Cabinet Secretariat in the event of a change of government. The Cabinet Secretary is custodian of Cabinet records for the government and previous governments; if required, Cabinet Secretariat will take over the management of Cabinet documents and issue detailed instructions for their return and lockdown.

Correspondence

Correspondence is an area where the need for agency judgement is once again identified. The principle for all jurisdictions is that correspondence should not be allowed to accumulate during the caretaker period. For practical reasons — mainly that ministers are usually busy or travelling for the campaign — there is general agreement they should only sign necessary correspondence. Agencies need to exercise judgement about whether correspondence is to be signed by the minister, CEO or another departmental officer. Most of the guidance documents focus on protecting the public service from any perception of partisanship. Details are given on avoiding the presumption that the government will be returned to office by referring to an 'incoming government'.

Public servants contesting elections

Not all jurisdictions cover this issue within their caretaker conventions; rather, it is generally the subject of a separate directive. Public servants have the same rights as other citizens to engage in the political process, though a range of considerations around impartiality and conflict of interest come into play if they do stand for office. The Commonwealth, Victoria, New South Wales, the Australian Capital Territory, Western Australia and the Northern Territory all warn that public officials should not use agency resources to support their personal political aspirations, and provide advice on how public speaking engagements should be managed.

The Queensland guidance states that public servants are entitled to contest state elections. They are not required to resign, but must take leave during the campaign. The details of managing leave provisions are subject to a separate directive. This process differs from the South Australian process, which requires officers to resign before the date of the declaration of the poll. If the candidate is unsuccessful, they can be reappointed and the break in service is deemed as leave without pay. Tasmanian candidates do not have to resign, and are entitled to leave without pay; however, if they are elected, their position is automatically terminated.

The Australian Constitution states that people cannot be chosen if they hold an office of profit under the Crown (s. 44 (iv)). Therefore, public servants — among others — must resign before nomination. But the *Public Service Act 1999* (Cth) (and the earlier 1922 Act) protects their positions if they are not successful (s. 32). This provision also applies when a public servant contests an election for a state parliament.

Other issues

A range of advice is given on issues that appear in a small number of jurisdictions, which may be a response to local controversies.

Grants

The Tasmanian, ACT and Northern Territory guidance documents all include a section on the management of grants during the caretaker period. All three jurisdictions advise that payment can be made on grants approved prior to the caretaker period, but should be forwarded by the department rather than the minister. No commitments should be made on grant applications received during the caretaker period.

Senior officials from several jurisdictions report that contracts and grants are especially sensitive when it seems likely the sitting government will be defeated and there is contention between the political parties about the agency or programs involved. Government-owned corporations, which are at arm's length from the core departments, but report to ministers and hence are bound by the caretaker conventions, are wise to exercise caution in the caretaker period, especially when their operations — or their mere existence — court controversy. Their obligations must be balanced against commercial considerations — such as, for example, where a delay would attract contract penalties or significantly disrupt a project that had been approved and already commenced.

Statutory authorities

The Northern Territory is the only jurisdiction that makes mention of the relationship between ministers and statutory authorities and/or government-owned corporations under a separate heading. The Commonwealth guidance mentions the relationship with statutory authorities as part of its Introduction. Both advise that the relationship between ministers and statutory authorities will vary depending on the body, but they recommend these bodies should observe caretaker conventions unless to do so would conflict with their legal obligations or commercial requirements.

Travel

Western Australia offers detailed advice on travel for Members of Parliament. It outlines who can travel, and under what circumstances, at state expense during the caretaker period. It is very prescriptive and even includes a formula for calculating the costs for media representatives travelling on charter flights. The Commonwealth and Victoria both cite the convention that ministers do not claim travel allowance from the day of the campaign launch to the day after polling day. The exception is if ministers have to travel for Cabinet meetings or in connection with their ministerial duties. The Victorian guidance also outlines the travel entitlements for the leaders of non-government parties once the election is called.

Tabling and responses to reports

The Commonwealth, Victorian, Tasmania and ACT guidance documents all cover the issue of formal responses to parliamentary reports. The advice is that outstanding reports should be taken up with the incoming government; however, in the meantime, agencies can undertake preparatory work and consultation at the agency level so they can provide early advice to the incoming government.

The Commonwealth and Victoria both advise that administrative reports, such as annual reports, can be tabled out of session. The Australian Capital Territory has a detailed framework for annual reporting, and makes specific provision for the timetable to present annual reports in an election year.

Conclusion

This detailed comparison of the caretaker provisions in all Australian jurisdictions exposes some interesting observations about management of the caretaker conventions. The tendency has been to add detail and advice as new issues emerge and need to be dealt with. Caretaker conventions were originally designed as a limited guidance for ministers on how to behave during an election campaign. The management of the updating of the guidances has since passed to the public service. Reflecting Australia's 'talent for bureaucracy', this transition has seen an increase in both the codification of behaviour and the complexity of the documents

The documents have also taken on a hybrid nature of providing advice to both ministers and public servants on how each should deal with the other during the caretaker period. Both sides seek to constrain the behaviour of each other, and this leads to some confusion as the guidances are giving advice for different audiences for particular issues. Despite increased codification, the real challenge in dealing with issues during the caretaker period still relies on judgement at both the political and public sector levels. Political judgement is required so as not to request the public service to undertake work that would compromise its impartiality. The public service must exercise judgement in ensuring it does not undertake work that would give the incumbent party an unfair advantage. The increase in prescriptive advice is an attempt to replace reliance on judgement with clear guidelines against which the behaviour of ministers and public servants can be acquitted. However, each election throws up new and unforseen challenges, and such an approach does not overcome the need for judgement to be exercised by senior staff.

Despite some local variations, the caretaker convention guidelines in all Australian jurisdictions remain clear about the principles behind the documents and the behaviour that derives from those principles. Given the caretaker period lasts for around 33 days every three to four years, the challenge for future versions is to maintain their intent and simplicity.

6. Caretaker Conventions: An Overview of New Zealand and Local Government Arrangements

The previous chapter presented a detailed analysis of the elements of the caretaker conventions in all Australian jurisdictions. This chapter will identify and explore the elements of the New Zealand and recent local government approaches.

New Zealand

In Chapter 3, we looked at the historical factors that drove the documentation of the New Zealand caretaker conventions. Adoption of the mixed member proportional electoral system (MMP) led to increased uncertainty and delay in the formation of new governments. The MMP system brought with it the potential for extended caretaker periods as the process of government formation could now be as lengthy as nine weeks, as the first MMP election demonstrated. These longer periods of transition from one government to the next have highlighted the need for greater prescription and codification. To respond to these changed circumstances, there was a consolidation and addition of advice to *The Cabinet Manual* after the 1996 election, and again in 2008.[1] In New Zealand, this trend was in response to a changed electoral system, while in Australia, greater prescription has largely been driven by a desire for rules and certainty about public service behaviour.

As in other Westminster-style systems, the principle behind the constraint imposed by the New Zealand caretaker convention is based on the sovereignty of Parliament and the recognition that, during the election period, the executive cannot be held accountable to the Parliament. The New Zealand convention is nevertheless quite clear that, in the pre-election period, the 'incumbent government is still the lawful executive authority, with all the powers and responsibilities that go with executive office' (NZDPM&C 2008, pp. 77–8). The key difference between the conventions of the Australian jurisdictions and New Zealand is the much greater focus on transitions and government formation after the election, and much less emphasis on detailed guidance on the management of issues during the actual election campaign. The Cabinet

---

1   *The Cabinet Manual* advises the need to plan ahead to try to ensure all significant matters are dealt with ahead of the election. Departments are warned that those who do not prepare for a protracted caretaker period are likely to experience problems.

Office and the State Services Commission issue guidance before each election to advise agencies on the principles applying during the pre- and post-election periods (New Zealand State Services Commission 2011).

The pre-election period

In New Zealand, the caretaker convention does not apply in the pre-election period (that is, the period of three months before polling day, or the period between election announcement and polling day if less than three months) unless the government has lost the confidence of the House. Successive governments have, however, chosen to restrict their actions in recognition that an election and potential change of government are imminent. During that time, restraint has been exercised in making significant appointments, and in relation to some government advertising (NZDPM&C 2008, p. 77). State officials are advised to work with Ministers at an early stage to agree to timeframes on progressing issues to Cabinet and finalising appointments (New Zealand Cabinet Office 2011).

The caretaker period

After the election, the caretaker convention applies. *The Cabinet Manual* outlines the different roles of departments, Crown entities and ministers during the caretaker period. It reconfirms the advice that the day-to-day administration of departments continues, and all issues with caretaker convention implications should be referred to the minister for a decision. A section reminds Crown entities and state-owned enterprises of their obligation to apply the principles of the caretaker period, taking into account their legal responsibilities and other statutory duties.

Responsibility for final decisions about the application of the caretaker convention rests with the Prime Minister, although preliminary assistance is available from the Secretary of the Cabinet. As well, the Prime Minister must be consulted on all issues that may require consultation with other political parties. The State Services Commission guidance offers advice on advertising and publicity campaigns, use of agency resources and contact with Members of Parliament. There is also detailed guidance on providing information during an election period and the need to meet the requirements of the *Official Information Act*. The guidance reminds public officials that requests for information made by political parties should be treated in the same way as any request for official information (NZSSC 2011, p. 12). This guidance was based on concerns raised by the Office of the Ombudsman after the 1990 election, where the Ombudsman was critical of state servants who had assessed the political consequences of releasing material rather than making the decision in a politically neutral manner (NZSSC 2011, p. 12). The Ombudsman found that the primary priority during an election campaign should be the speedy release of material and the 'extreme importance of a well-informed electorate' (NZSSC 2011, p. 23).

Detailed work has been undertaken on the procedures for the costing of both government and Opposition policies. The bureaucracy must receive a written request from the Minister of Finance or the department's minister before any work can be undertaken. All work, including sources and procedures, must be documented in full and no additional commentary or subjective assumptions are allowed. The costing guidelines confirm that ministers 'will not require or use information on costings in a way that might damage the neutrality of the State Services, and hence its ability to serve successive governments' (SSC 2011, p. 19).

Transitional arrangements

Experience in New Zealand has led to detailed clarification of the principles involved in managing the interregnum after the election before a new government is formed. There are 'two arms' to the convention:

- where it is not clear who will form the next government
- where it is clear who will form the next government, but they have not yet taken office (NZDPM&C 2008, p. 78).

When it is clear who will form the next government, the incumbent but outgoing government should avoid undertaking any new policy initiatives and act on the advice of the incoming government on any matters of significance — even if the outgoing government disagrees with the course of action. As we saw in Chapter 3, this formulation is a direct response to the crisis of 1984.

The second 'arm' of advice, concerning how to manage when it is not clear who will form the next government, is more detailed — a consequence of the length of time before a government could be formed after the 1996 election. Confusion around what the outgoing government could and could not do led to development of two principles, which are:

- decisions taken and specific policy determined before the start of the caretaker period may be implemented by a caretaker government, and
- in general terms, the normal business of government and the day-to-day administration of departments and agencies in the wider state sector may continue during the caretaker period (NZDPM&C 2008, p. 78).

However, it is recommended that a range of decisions around significant issues that might bind an incoming government should be deferred, be handled by temporary arrangements or be subject to consultation with other parties. *The Cabinet Manual* stresses the need for careful judgement by ministers, public servants and Crown entities, and does acknowledge there are no 'hard and fast rules' (NZDPM&C 2008, p. 79), and a range of considerations will need to be taken into account before a decision is made.

Government formation

A large proportion of *The Cabinet Manual* guidance concerns the process for the formation of a new government. It is the Governor-General's role to ascertain where the confidence of the House lies, based on the parties' public statements, so that a government can be appointed. As part of that process, negotiating parties may seek advice from the public service, and departmental officials may provide that advice if authorised to do so by the Prime Minister. Detailed advice for public sector officials on how to manage those negotiations is published by the New Zealand State Services Commission (2008). This guidance sets out the arrangements under which parties negotiating to form a government are able to access information and analysis from government departments. The State Services Commissioner is the contact point for receiving and responding to these requests.

These instructions are detailed, and set out the different responsibilities for critical public sector employees such as the Chief Executive of the Department of the Prime Minister and Cabinet, the Cabinet Secretary and the Secretary to the Treasury. The Clerk of the Executive Council is responsible for providing impartial support to the Governor-General, while the State Services Commissioner keeps the Prime Minister informed about what assistance is being given to different political parties. There is extreme sensitivity about the provision of information and analysis to political parties, and this is reflected in the requirement that only a small number of senior officials be involved to apply both 'judgement and discretion' (NZSSC 2011, p. 3).

The material provided on caretaker conventions in New Zealand is detailed and promulgated in advance of each election. This has arisen because of the electoral uncertainty that now exists under the MMP system, and the potential for an extended caretaker period for government formation following polling day.

This flurry of documentation from the 1990s reflected the transition from a long period of single-party majority governments to majority and minority coalition governments (Boston et al. 1998, p. 648). The introduction of MMP saw a rapid increase in detail on how to manage issues in a time of increased uncertainty, particularly after elections. That advice has been refined after the past couple of elections, and now offers a detailed guide for the incumbent party, the incoming government (in the event of a change) and the public service on how to handle itself in unsettled times.

Local government in Australia

In recent times, the majority of jurisdictions in Australia have enacted caretaker provisions within their *Local Government Acts*, first introduced by Victoria in 2003 and Queensland in 2007. These new statutory arrangements derived from concerns about official misconduct and the integrity of practices during local council elections. In Victoria, the change to the legislation was a response to a review of the state constitution in 2003. In Queensland, the legislation was in response to a Crime and Misconduct Commission (CMC 2006) report into the conduct of candidates at the 2004 Gold Coast City Council elections. Like the state and Commonwealth conventions, the local government arrangements are concerned with curtailing the benefits of incumbency and preventing the present administration from making decisions that would commit an incoming council. The arrangements are based on the caretaker principle that every election brings the possibility of a change of government. Making the provisions legally binding has a number of implications, which are explored below.

The main focus of local government caretaker requirements is to prevent inappropriate decision-making by councils during an election period, and to ensure council resources are not being used to support the activities of existing councillors, with a particular emphasis on the publication of electoral matter. Individual councils are required to develop a caretaker policy to govern the conduct of both staff and councillors before an election. The various *Local Government Acts* specify a range of decisions that council may not take during an election period. In general, the provisions prevent:

- appointing or terminating a CEO or changing the remuneration of a CEO (this clause also has implications for other senior executives)
- entering into contracts valued at more than $100,000 (New South Wales and Victoria) or $150,000 (Queensland and South Australia) or valued at more than 1 per cent of the council's revenue from rates (whichever is the greater)
- determining a controversial development application
- the use of council resources for publications that advantage a candidate or group of candidates.

State jurisdictions provide an option for ministerial appeal in exceptional circumstances. If the local council believes a major policy decision is required in the public interest, it can apply to the minister for approval to make the decision. If such an approval is not received, the contracts and decisions are invalid. Because most of the legislation is recent, the implications for breaches are as yet untested, as is the potential for ministerial involvement in making judgements about alleged breaches. The introduction of four-year terms for most local councils allows for an orderly management of council business in the run-up to an election. Combined with the community-based rather than partisan alignment of most local government candidates, this has meant major breaches have not been a feature of recent council elections.

Legislating caretaker conventions in local government – unintended consequences?

The recent adoption by state jurisdictions of legislated caretaker arrangements have had a number of consequences. The state *Local Government Acts* are based on the same formula and bring local government into line with state and Commonwealth practices. The legislation of caretaker arrangements for councils is still in its early days, but it is possible to conceive of a range of complexities that could arise in the face of such a legalistic approach.

Local government representatives in Australia tend to be community representatives rather than organised along party lines. This could lead to fewer constraints on behaviour, as there is often no party machine to exercise discipline and set standards of electoral behaviour. Hence the recent trend to legislate caretaker behaviour could be a response to the lack of political sanctions that would normally operate against a political party seen to flaunt the caretaker provisions. A legislated response puts the onus back on individual behaviour instead of the mutually agreed responsibility which is the hallmark of a convention.

The role of the Local Government Minister as decision-maker has the potential for conflict, particularly if there are partisan differences between the two jurisdictions. There is the potential for claims of breaches to be tested in the courts, particularly around definitions of what is a 'major policy decision' and 'election matter'. The legislation is silent on whether council officers can be prosecuted for breaches, and it does not identify whether it is the CEO or the Lord Mayor who is the accountable officer for implementing and managing these arrangements during the caretaker period. The caretaker arrangements focus on limiting the advantages of incumbency but do not formalise the rights of the opposing candidates to access briefings from the administration.

Compared with the more detailed guidance documents of the other levels of Australian and New Zealand governments, the legislation is short on detail and nuances. This lack of information could leave the legislation open to challenge and legal interpretation. Legislation is a blunt tool, and by legislating these arrangements local government loses some of the evolutionary capacity and flexibility that a non-legislated convention gives. Legislation is time-consuming and difficult to update, and cannot easily reflect the nuances of changing practice. A self-managed process retains the capacity for regular updating to respond to local circumstances and issues as they arise.

Conclusion

This chapter completes the detailed analysis of the different approaches to caretaker conventions in all Australian jurisdictions, including local government and New Zealand. The likelihood of a publicised breach or confused response during the heat of an election campaign drives the continued updating of prescriptive guidance documents. Constitutional crises in New Zealand have now led to multiple sources of advice for the executive government, the Governor-General, minority parties and the public sector.

Support for the observance of caretaker conventions for local governments is less institutionalised — presumably because it is a comparatively recent development. Local councils are improving their internal support for managing their caretaker provisions as the legislated implications of real or perceived breaches increase the onus on them to support their officials during this time.

7. Forces Influencing the Observance of Caretaker Conventions

The cases and controversies highlighted in earlier chapters have much to tell us about the pressures on the interpretation of caretaker conventions, and the sensitive issues that public officials must navigate when upholding caretaker principles during an election campaign and until the swearing in of a new government. This chapter highlights some of the dilemmas posed by the need to be responsive to government while remaining apolitical, and upholding public service obligations to be professional, impartial and to comply with the law. It addresses some of the forces impinging on public service impartiality.

Adversarialism and partisan contest

Arguably, some of the anxiety surrounding caretaker conventions relates to the competitive and intensely partisan environment of contemporary politics. Although we live in an era of the 'permanent campaign', the period leading up to polling day is especially fraught — ministers and their staff are under intense pressure; Opposition spokespeople are looking to exploit opportunities to secure political advantage; journalists are looking to break controversial stories and to 'get behind' tightly stage-managed 'run of the mill' announcements. The public service sometimes becomes collateral damage in these relentless quests, which may be why public service leaders have seemed more willing in recent times to 'go public' to explain the basis of their advice and decisions during the caretaker period. When it is anticipated that a sitting government will be defeated, Opposition parties seem especially keen to remind the public service of its obligations to be impartial — the inference being that a negative consequence might flow for a career official seen as too responsive to the current government, rather than to the new administration likely to be formed after the election.

As guidance documents make clear, decisions about whether caretaker conventions have been breached are ultimately matters for Prime Ministers and Premiers. They make political calculations about the benefits and risks of particular courses of action. Although it is relatively common for someone to claim that caretaker conventions have been breached, such claims are rarely substantiated. Usually the public debate moves on, or investigations reveal that the decision taken in the matter was a question of judgment. Caretaker guidance documents are guidances only — not hard and fast rules. But, as cases and examples canvassed in this volume have shown, adversarial partisan politics is challenging traditional understandings of conventions as shared norms of behaviour. It creates particular strains on those aspects of the conventions where consultation with the Opposition is required.

Has 'hyper-partisanship' become the new normal?

The 2010 federal election delivered a hung parliament for the first time in Australia since 1941. Labor and the Coalition won 72 seats each at the federal poll of August 2013. The incumbent Prime Minister successfully negotiated an agreement with the Australian Greens and three regional Independents to form a minority government. The Coalition's frustration at having fallen just short of forcing a change of government was palpable. It believed Gillard's precarious alliance could fracture at any time. Journalist David Marr (2012, p. 64) reported:

> The Opposition was led by a man who believed that at any moment death, scandal or defection could make him Prime Minister. He was intent on demolishing the government and wrecking the parliament. But it didn't happen, despite the scandals laid on by the Labor Party. The parliament functioned. Gillard survived. Complex legislation was passed. And month in, month out, pollsters reported that Australians were loathing it all: minority government, the taxes, the tone of national debate ...

Some analysts argue the 'hyper-partisanship' that characterised the minority federal government from 2010–13 has become the modus operandi of contemporary politics — in Australian jurisdictions, at least. Jim Chalmers, a former Labor Chief of Staff and now the Member for the federal seat of Rankin, argues that 'badly misaligned incentives in our political system ... tilt the playing field in favour of the new hyper-partisans', who he defines as 'extremists on the Left and Right who prioritise combat over problem-solving'. He argues that, 'The most blatantly partisan political actors are not only found in the parliaments but also in journalism, the public affairs branches of our major peak organisations, lobbying houses and the broader commentariat.' (Chalmers 2013, pp. 104–5) The heated atmosphere of an election campaign is especially ripe for the often-confected outrage of those less interested in substantive issues and responsibilities than the drive to win and retain power.

Pressures on public service responsiveness

The public service is expected to be responsive to the government it serves. In most jurisdictions, the public service values and codes of conduct are explicit on this point. The obligation to be professional, neutral and impartial, and at the same time to serve the government of the day, continues during the caretaker period. Tensions about this balance can become an issue with ministerial offices, which are accustomed to a different relationship with the bureaucracy. Often, these can be dealt with by establishing agreed protocols at the commencement of the caretaker period. In preparing for recent federal elections, the Department of the Prime Minister and Cabinet has conducted briefing sessions for chiefs of staff on the caretaker conventions and what it is reasonable for their ministers to expect by way of advice and support during the caretaker period.

Ministerial staff

Ministerial staff play important roles in ensuring public service responsiveness to ministers and to the policy directions of government (Tiernan 2007; Tiernan and Weller 2010). The growth in their numbers and reach has created new challenges for public servants during the caretaker period. The potential for staff to make inappropriate or unreasonable requests of departments is occasionally highlighted in articles about the caretaker period (Malone 2007; Owens 2012) and was clearly evident in the 'Children Overboard' case, which unfolded in the partisan glare of the 2001 federal election (Tiernan 2007; Weller 2002).

In the Victorian case, Davis et al. (2001, p. 19) note the tensions public servants faced as they sought to remain politically impartial while dealing with ministerial advisers 'whose main objectives were overtly political'. They note the conventions are 'silent on the role of political advisers during the caretaker period' (Davis et al. 2001, p. 20). Former Deputy Prime Minister Brian Howe (2001, p. 28) notes that 'advisers have become essential when ministers/shadow ministers need to understand points of difference in technical detail likely to arise during an extended caretaker period', but he concedes their unelected and unaccountable status raises issues when they represent their principals in negotiations.

Given the potential for ministerial staff to conduct themselves in ways that are not strictly in accordance with the spirit of the caretaker conventions, Keating (2002, p. 120) suggests that public servants should insist on directly briefing the minister or shadow minister during the caretaker period, and ensure that their personal agreement is obtained for any unavoidable decision taken. This recommendation would essentially place the responsibility for initiating contact with either the government and/or the Opposition in an election context on public servants — a situation that would pose considerable difficulties for all but the most senior officials.

Former PM&C Secretary Terry Moran, who previously served as Secretary of the Victorian Department of the Premier and Cabinet, agrees staffers have become a 'big problem':

> The reason for that is that the old conventions governing their roles no longer hold true ... There is insufficient accountability because there are so many ministerial advisers now with few, in some jurisdictions, who actually possess a grasp of the business of government commensurate with their responsibilities. No one can suggest that they are an expression of the 'persona' of the minister any more. Now the minister isn't accountable for what they do, because now a minister can say, 'Oh that was one of my advisers, I did not know about this.' (quoted in Alford 2012)

Others reject this blanket characterisation of ministerial staffers, noting that relationships are more cooperative than frequent criticisms would allow. For example, an experienced senior official argued that during a recent election, chiefs of staff were right to raise concerns about why some departments were not processing grants or contracts that had been determined and approved prior to the commencement of the caretaker period. They were justified in questioning why public servants were not implementing government policy. He attributed public servants' reticence to the widespread belief that the government would be defeated at the forthcoming elections. Officials seemed especially concerned about matters that were contentious with the Opposition. They didn't want to be criticised, or be in the situation shortly afterwards of having to extract the Commonwealth from a commitment not supported by an incoming government. Public servants are by nature cautious, he explained; they are anxious to avoid controversy. They want to preserve their capacity to build effective working relationships with an incoming minister and their staff.

This echoes concerns expressed by staffers in Commonwealth and state jurisdictions about a lack of responsiveness from departments when it appears the end of a government is nigh. The principle that the government remains the government until the end of the caretaker period is clear, and officials would do well to remember that partisans can have long memories and that the experience of a lack of responsiveness could affect relationships of trust into the future.

Good practitioners on both sides of the political–administrative divide recognise such difficulties can be avoided by ensuring only the most senior and experienced officials are responsible for managing the interface with ministers and the Opposition as the alternative government during the caretaker period. Recent guidance documents have recommended agencies appoint internal experts to handle queries. These officers can then be the conduit for advice and support from central agency experts on difficult or sensitive issues that might arise, or are of concern.

In many ways, the Commonwealth Government practice of ministerial staff decamping from Canberra to campaign offices in Sydney or Melbourne may relieve some of the demands on public servants. In state governments, where ministerial offices are often co-located with departments, the challenge may be greater, but accountability and oversight regimes for ministerial staff are comparatively stronger in Australian state jurisdictions than in the Commonwealth.

Technological change

As noted in previous chapters, technological change — notably the rise of the internet and email, as well as social media — has necessitated the development of new practices and guidance to assist public servants to manage within the spirit and intent of the caretaker conventions. The implications of technological change was not canvassed in earlier iterations of the guidance documents, and issues of government websites simply did not arise. The 2004 guidance document gave agency heads discretion to determine their own portfolio's approach to websites. This attracted some criticism. Malone (2007, p. 4) has called for stronger prescription and consistency to assist public servants in maintaining their impartiality during the caretaker period. Such developments would further reinforce the tendency to bureaucratise caretaker conventions.

Pace and complexity of decision-making

The increased pace and complexity of government decision-making is much remarked upon by practitioners and scholars. An uncertain international security and threat environment has added to this complexity, creating demands for governments to take decisive action even during election campaigns. Controversy followed the Howard government's decision to deploy an SAS hostage crisis team to Iraq in 2004, and there were questions about the government's use of the military in its Pacific Solution policy during the 2001 federal election. In 2004, the Australian embassy in Jakarta was bombed; the attack occurred during the caretaker period. Because governments need to move quickly in such situations, academic John Uhr (in AAP, 15 September 2004) has argued there may be a need for 'supplementary rules' to guide crisis decision-making.

Power of incumbency

During long periods of incumbency, ministers and their staffs become accustomed to the high levels of support provided by departments. Depending on their level of experience, ministers and members of their staff may find it difficult to adjust to the reduced levels of assistance with advice and briefing from officials. Recent research indicates that the average period of incumbency is 11.6 years for governments federally, and just under eleven years in state jurisdictions (Strangio 2006). In office, governments enjoy substantial advantages in terms of staffing and resources, and the capacity to use advertising and other political 'weapons' in their efforts to retain elected office. The likelihood that a serving government will be returned may create difficulties for public servants in 'standing up' to a minister or their staff over a caretaker conventions issue.

Conclusion

A number of forces in modern politics influence the interpretation and management of government business during the caretaker period. This chapter has identified the pressures that greater adversarialism, the growth in power and influence of ministerial staff, rapid technological change, the pace and complexity of decision-making and the power of incumbency are placing on public servants during election campaigns. These influences are driving the trend to codification and bureaucratisation of guidance documents on caretaker conventions, and have been influential in shifting the onus of responsibility to observe the conventions from ministers to bureaucrats.

These forces — particularly the trend from the old style parliamentarianism, where pleasantries could be exchanged across the House, to the professionalism of party machine politics — have led to a more ruthless approach to maximising political advantage. The next chapter explores some of the consequences this transformation could have on caretaker conventions.

8. Caretaker Conventions and the Future of Responsible Government

The scope and application of caretaker conventions will continue to evolve. In previous chapters, we documented the similarities and differences between the jurisdictions under consideration, and looked at the implications of changing practice.

Caretaker conventions are among the most challenged and controversial of all conventions. They apply during the most intense time of adversarial politics: when both major parties have the potential to retain or gain government. Minor slips and inexactitudes are exploited by both sides. There is intense pressure on public servants to justify their decisions regarding perceived support or partiality for the incumbent government. As outlined in Chapter 2, conventions are about a shared understanding of and mutual responsibility for their upkeep. Perhaps the nature of modern adversarial politics gives the concept of conventions a somewhat antiquated air. The introduction of ministerial codes of conduct and anti-corruption commissions indicates political participants appear less trusting of mutuality, and they are becoming more interested in enforceable sanctions.

An important corollary of this development is whether the voluntary nature of caretaker conventions can be sustained in contemporary politics? Caretaker conventions were established on the principle of 'self-policing', but as accusations intensify about alleged government breaches of conventions, might not future governments consider establishing an independent arbiter? A transition from the status of convention to a set of legally enforceable rules would see a radical recasting of caretaker arrangements.

Prescription and codification

It is difficult to pinpoint precisely when the maintenance of caretaker conventions shifted from being a political responsibility to a primarily bureaucratic one. In his 1951 letter to ministers, Prime Minister Menzies was clear it was their responsibility to exercise judgement in the continuing operation of their departments. As this monograph has demonstrated, a simple letter reminding ministers of their responsibilities has been, since the 1970s, supplanted by increasingly detailed guidance designed to support public servants to make decisions across a broad range of government activities. Jurisdictions now review their guidance documents after each election to respond to recent controversies or ambiguities. This has led to a pattern of increasing prescription and specification as jurisdictions try to prevent repetition of claimed breaches and controversies by increasing or adding new suggestions about how to handle a particular situation.

The guidances have evolved into strangely hybrid documents. They acknowledge the responsibility of government politicians to adhere to the conventions — for example, 'adherence to the conventions is ultimately the responsibility of the Premier and the Government collectively' (Vic DPC 2010, p. 6). Yet the advice contained is focused on assisting the public sector to put boundaries around and manage the relationship with their political masters. An example of this can be seen in the Victorian guidance document, which describes the established practices around caretaker conventions aimed at 'protecting the apolitical nature of the VPS and avoiding the use of State resources to advantage a particular political party' (Vic DPC 2010, p. 6). During the 2013 federal election, the Secretaries of the Departments of the Prime Minister and Cabinet, Treasury and Finance all publicly published material to defend their actions and the impartiality of their respective departments during the campaign.[1]

Increasing prescription has the potential to diminish bi-partisan agreement on the caretaker conventions. If conventions are mutually agreed principles that guide political behaviour, that mutuality may be eroded by incumbents adding new levels of detail to the guidance documents. Quite often, the updating is undertaken at a bureaucratic level, as officers try to counteract criticism by adding advice on how to manage, for example, the impact of the internet. To preserve the mutuality of caretaker conventions, amendments should be agreed by both major political parties to ensure the acceptance of bi-partisan responsibility for their maintenance and observance.

Codification and prescription also lead to a focus on interpretation and a loss of flexibility. An emerging concern is that increased prescription will lead to legal sanctions for breaches for the public service. Codification also shifts the responsibility to adhere to the restraints away from politicians and displaces it on to the public service. The public sector's tendency to document and regulate might, in the longer term, transfer the spotlight from political behaviour to bureaucratic interpretation and application. This is already evident in some of the commentary on caretaker conventions (see, for example, Malone 2007).

---

[1] PM&C Secretary Ian Watt made public correspondence between himself and Opposition Leader Tony Abbott on the 'By Boat, No Visa' campaign and on the signing of the Memorandum of Understanding between Australia and Papua New Guinea on the resettlement of refugees. Secretaries Martin Parkinson and David Tune released a media release denying that either the Treasury or Department of Finance and Deregulation had costed Opposition policies.

The introduction of statutory sets of public service values and codes of conduct means that public servants now have legal obligations for non-partisan behaviour, and these apply during the caretaker period. This was tested by a Queensland Crime and Misconduct Commission Inquiry in 2004, which found – though the conventions were not legally binding on politicians – a different standard applied to public servants who were bound by the principle of impartiality contained in their *Public Service Act 1996* (Qld) (CMC 2004, pp. 26–7).[2] Although it has not been repeated since, the potential remains for public servants to be caught in similar breaches, with the possibility that disciplinary or financial sanctions could be applied. The implication is clear, although little publicised at present. Public servants are exposed in ways that ministers still are not. This changing environment will only accelerate the trend to prescription to be used as a bulwark against ministerial demands for responsiveness during the caretaker period.

Future prospects

If a convention reflects shared norms about political behaviour, is it not the prerogative of the government of the day to update or revise its content or application? Over the years, public servants have unobtrusively become the guardians of the detail and the application of the caretaker conventions. The continuing declining trust in politicians could contribute to this trend. Surveys show the perception of the ethical standards and honesty of politicians continues to decline.[3] As the management of conventions is about trust and ethical standards, as trust diminishes in the capacity of politicians to self-police, a greater emphasis is placed on written codes and external regulation bodies to administer its application. This presents a dilemma because public servants understandably want the certainty and clarity that detailed procedures provide. Australia's 'talent for bureaucracy' (Davies 1964) tends to favour addressing problems by the development of detailed guidelines and procedures.

The trend to increased codification could reflect a diminished understanding of, and experience with, the processes of government. In the past, the application of conventions has been the province of the most senior bureaucrats. Their long experience and judgement allowed them to make the fine distinctions often required to navigate the political–public service interface. To do so successfully

---

2   The Queensland Crime and Misconduct Commission report The Tugun Bypass Investigation looked into a complaint by the then Leader of the Opposition that officers of the Department of Main Roads were 'acting in a politically partisan manner to implement a major Government decision during an election campaign' (CMC 2004, p. 7).
3   The 2013 Roy Morgan Survey of the perceptions of ethical standards of professions shows the standing of both state and federal politicians continues to decline, with only 14 per cent thinking they have high standards (Roy Morgan 2013).

requires a capacity to apply the caretaker principles with the confidence to take and defend such judgements in the contested atmosphere of an election campaign. Arguably, contemporary trends in public sector employment — rapid progression to senior ranks, external appointments to senior positions and greater use of contract appointments — could account for uncertainty and discomfort in applying the caretaker conventions. If that is the case, the trend to codification and prescription is likely to continue so that senior officials can point to written guidance as the basis for their decision-making.

The controversy that surrounds the application of caretaker conventions is unlikely to diminish, but political processes require political solutions. The increase in detail in the application of caretaker conventions cannot continue indefinitely, and eventually responsibility will have to return to ministers and political leaders to manage. With the increased potential for public servants to be disciplined for breaches of the guidelines, there might well be some relief in returning ownership to the political players.

Glossary

Cabinet A committee of ministers that forms the apex of executive decision-making.

Charter of Budget Honesty An Act that provides, among other things, for a pre-election costing of government and Opposition commitments and policies during the caretaker period. The charter is the subject of significant controversy.

Constitution The set of rules by which a country or state is governed. In Australia, the Constitution was written in the 1890s and it sets out the structure of Australian federal government and its relationship to the states. The Constitution can only be explicitly amended by referendum.

Convention Non-legal rules that guide political practice in areas on which the Constitution is silent.

Dissolution of the House of Representatives The House of Representatives is dissolved by the Governor-General under mechanisms specified in the Constitution (ss. 5 and 57).

Double dissolution Colloquial term for dissolution of both the Senate and the House of Representatives arising when the Senate blocks, fails to pass or amends a Bill unacceptably on two occasions with a gap of at least three months.

Executive Council A committee of the Governor-General or Governor meeting with members of the Cabinet. Governor-General-in-Council/Governor-in-Council gives legal effect to many of the decisions of government, such as subordinate legislation and appointments.

Mixed Member Proportional (MMP) electoral system The New Zealand electoral system, introduced in 1996, is based on each elector having two votes — one for a party and one for a local candidate.

Prorogation of Parliament A discontinuation of a session of Parliament without dissolving it.

Royal Assent The Governor-General or Governor gives assent to laws when they have been passed by Parliament. This is the final step in the legislative process, with assent giving legal effect to Bills — which then become Acts.

Subordinate legislation Legislation that does not need to be enacted through Parliament and made under the authority of existing Acts. Material that might form the basis of subordinate legislation includes by-laws, orders, ordinances, statutory instruments and notices. Subordinate legislation is signed off by the Governor-General/Governor-in-Council.

Westminster government The Westminster model of government is based on practices of the British government, with such practices being adopted by a range of representative democracies. Elements of the Westminster model include: parliamentary sovereignty; a collective and responsible Cabinet; ministers accountable to Parliament; a non-partisan and permanent civil service; and an Opposition recognised as an executive-in-waiting.

Writ A document commanding an electoral officer to hold an election. The writ contains dates for the close of rolls, the close of nominations, election day and the return of the writ.

References

ABC News 2013, 'ABC's Barrie Cassidy quits Old Parliament advisory council amid pressure form Attorney-General George Brandis', 25 October, http://www.abc.net.au/news/2013-10-25/brandis-asks-cassidy-to-quit-old-parliament-advisory-council/5044882, accessed 10 January 2014.

AAP 2004, 'Hill says Iraq plan not covered by caretaker rule', Australian Associated Press, 16 September.

Abbott, T. 2013a, *Communication — 6 August*.

—— 2013b, *Communication — 9 August*, http://www.dpmc.gov.au/media/communication_2013-08-11.cfm, accessed 10 January 2014.

Alford, J. 2012, 'Terry Moran in conversation', *The Conversation*, 1 November, theconversation.edu.au/terry-moran-in-conversation-full-transcript-101873/7, accessed 10 January 2014.

Australian Capital Territory (ACT) 2012, *Guidance on Caretaker Conventions*, ACT Government, September.

Australian Government Information Management Office (AGIMO) 2013, *Caretaker 2013: Only Talking Business as Usual*, http://www.finance.gov.au/blog/2013/08/05/caretaker-2013-%E2%80%93-only-talking-business-usual, accessed 20 February 2014.

Australian Public Service Commission (APSC) 2006, *Supporting Ministers: Upholding the Values — A Good Practice Guide*, Australian Public Service Commission, Canberra.

—— 2012, *Circular 2012/1: Revisions to the Commission's Guidance on Making Public Comment and Participating Online*, http://www.apsc.gov.au/publications-and-media/current-circulars-and-advices/2012/circular-20121, accessed 20 February 2014.

Boston, J., Levine, S., McLeay, E., Roberts, N. and Schmidt, H. 1998, 'Caretaker government and the evolution of caretaker conventions in New Zealand', *Victoria University of Wellington Law Review*, 28(4), 629–48.

Bourke, L. 2013, 'Education minister Peter Garrett banned from Queensland schools in row over Gonski funding', *ABC News*, 12 June, http://www.abc.net.au/news/2013-06-12/education-minister-peter-garrett-banned-from-Queensland-schools/4747868, accessed 20 July 2013.

Brandis, J. 2013 Media release, 'Mr Barrie Cassidy', 25 October, http://www.attorneygeneral.gov.au/Mediareleases/Pages/2013/Fourth%20quarter/25October2013-MrBarrieCassidy.aspx.

Canberra Times 2004, 'Propaganda Pays Off', Editorial, 24 October.

Chalmers, J. 2013, *Glory Daze: How a World-beating Nation Got So Down on Itself*, Melbourne University Press, Melbourne.

Charlton, P. 2001,'Caretaker's Conundrum', *Courier-Mail* (Brisbane), 9 October.

Codd, M. 1996, 'National elections: Caretaker conventions and arrangements for transition', Australian Institute of Administrative Law (AIAL) Forum No. 10.

Colebatch, H. 2005, 'A "talent for bureaucracy": A.F. Davies and the Analysis of government in Australia', *Australian Journal of Public Administration*, 64(4), 32–40.

Cooray, L.J.M. 1979, *Conventions, the Australian Constitution and the Future*, Legal Books, Sydney.

Crime and Misconduct Commission (CMC) 2004, *The Tugan Bypass Investigation*, Crime and Misconduct Commission Report.

—— 2006, *Independence, Influence and Integrity in Local Government: A CMC Inquiry into the 2004 Gold Coast Election*, Crime and Misconduct Commission Report.

Crowe, D. 2013, 'Tony Abbott risks Treasury ire on costings claim'. *The Australian*, 31 August.

Davies, A.F. 1964, *Australian Democracy: An Introduction to the Political System*, Longmans, Green, Melbourne.

Davis, G., Ling, A., Scales, B. and Wilkins, R. 2001, 'Rethinking caretaker conventions for Australian governments', *Australian Journal of Public Administration*, 60(3), 11–26.

Department of Defence 2014, Media Release, 8 September.

Department of Finance and Deregulation 2012, *Charter of Budget Honesty Policy Costings Guidelines:Guidelines Issued Jointly by the Secretaries to the Treasury and the Department of Finance and Deregulation*, Commonwealth of Australia, Canberra, http://www.finance.gov.au/publications/charter-of-budget-honesty/index.html, accessed 20 September 2013.

Department of the Prime Minister and Cabinet (DPM&C) 1987, 'Caretaker conventions and other pre-election practices', *Annual Report 1986–87*, AGPS, Canberra.

—— 2010, *Guidelines for Post-election Consultations with Independent Members*, AGPS, Canberra.

—— 2013, *Guidance on Caretaker Conventions*, Department of the Prime Minister and Cabinet, Canberra.

Dicey, A.V. 1959, *An Introduction to the Study of the Law of the Constitution*, 10th ed., Macmillan, London.

The Drum 2013, 'Opposition claims asylum ads 'unlawful' as government continues $30 million campaign during caretaker period', http://thedrum. com.news/201308/opposition-claims-asylum-ads-unlawful-government-continues-30-million-campaign, accessed 20 January 2014.

Finance & Public Administration (F&PA) Committee 2002, *Committee Hansard*, Senate Finance and Public Administration Committee, May.

—— 2013, *Committee Hansard*, Senate Finance and Public Administration Committee, 18 November.

Gosch, E. 2001, 'Thirty-ninth parliament dissolved ahead of November 10 election', Australian Associated Press, 9 October.

Gustafson, B. 2000, *His Way: A Biography of Robert Muldoon*, Auckland University Press, Auckland.

Hasluck, P. 1979, *The Office of Govenor-General*, Melbourne University Press, Melbourne.

Hawker, G. and Weller, P. 1974, 'Pre-election consultations: A proposal and its problems', *Australian Quarterly*, 46(2), 100–4.

Heard, A. 1991, *Canadian Constitutional Conventions: The Marriage of Law and Politics*, Oxford University Press, Toronto.

Hood Phillips, O. and Jackson, P. 1978, *Constitutional and Administrative Law*, 6th ed., Sweet and Maxwell, London.

Howe, B. 2001, 'Comment on "Rethinking caretaker conventions for Australian governments"', *Australian Journal of Public Administration*, 60(3), 27–8.

Hughes, C. and Costar, B. 2006, *Limiting Democracy: The Erosion of Electoral Rights in Australia*, UNSW Press, Sydney.

Jaconelli, J. 2005, 'Do constitutional conventions bind?' *Cambridge Law Journal*, 64(1), March, pp 149-176.

Jennings, I. 1959, *The Law and the Constitution*, 5th ed., University of London Press, London.

Kane, J. 2006, 'Constitutionalising local government', *Public Administration Today,* July–September, pp. 24–6.

Keating, M. 2002, 'Caretaker conventions post an election', *Australian Journal of Public Administration*, 61(2), 119–20.

Kenny, C. 2013, 'Labor's secret job offer for Barrie Cassidy', *The Australian*, 23 October.

Kenny, M. 2013, 'Treasury deny any part in calculating Coalition's $10b savings hole', *Sydney Morning Herald*, 30 August.

Kerin, J. 2004, 'Direct hit on Hill's use of site', *The Australian*, 9 September.

Kitney, G. and Maley, K. 1993, 'Keating claims health victory', *Sydney Morning Herald*, 9 February.

Laver, K. and Schepsle, A. 1994, *Cabinet Ministers and Parliamentary Government: The Political Economy of Institutions and Decisions*, Cambridge University Press, Melbourne.

Lindell, G.J. 1988, 'Executive actions and appointments following a dissolution of parliament', *Australian Law Journal*, 62, 321–2.

Malone, P. 2007, 'Time to tighten the caretaker conventions', Democratic Audit of Australia Discussion Paper 3/07, February.

Marshall, G 1984, *Constitutional Conventions: The Rules and Forms of Political Accountability*, Clarendon Press, Oxford.

—— 2004, 'The Constitution: Its theory and interpretation', in V. Bognador (ed.), *The British Constitution in the Twentieth Century*, Oxford University Press, Oxford.

Marshall, G. and Moodie, G. 1971, *Some Problems of the Constitution*, 5th ed., Hutchinson University Library, London.

Marr, D. 2012, 'Political animal: The making of Tony Abbott', *Quarterly Essay*, 47.

Marr, D. and Wilkinson, M. 2003, *Dark Victory*, Allen & Unwin, Sydney.

McLeay, E. 1999, 'What is the constitutional status of the New Zealand *Cabinet Office Manual?' Public Law Review*, 10, 11–17.

McMullan, B. 2007, 'The dangers of complacency: The case for reforming fiscal policy in Australia', in J. Wanna (ed.), *A Passion for Policy: Essays in Public Sector Reform*, ANU E Press, Canberra.

Morozow, A. 2013, '"Asylum seeker policy ads fine to run during election campaign", Auditor-General rules', *ABC News*, 15 August.

New South Wales Department of Premier and Cabinet (NSWDPC) 2011, *Caretaker Conventions and Other Pre-election Practices: 2011 General State Election*, NSW Government, Sydney.

New South Wales Government 2012, *Advertising Handbook*, http://www.advertising.nsw.gov.au, accessed 20 February 2013.

New Zealand Cabinet Office 2011, 'Government decisions and actions in the pre-election period', Circular (11)2.

New Zealand Department of the Prime Minister and Cabinet (NZDMP&C) 2008, *Cabinet Manuel*, NZPM&C, Wellington.

New Zealand State Services Commission (NZSSC) 2008, *Negotiations Between Political Parties to Form a Government: Guidelines on Support from the State Sector*, New Zealand Government, Wellington.

—— 2011, *State Servants, Political Parties and Elections: Guidance for the 2011 Election Period*, New Zealand Government, Wellington.

Northern Territory Department of the Chief Minister (NTDCM) 2012, *Guidance on Caretaker Conventions*, NT Government, Darwin.

Odgers Australian Guide to Senate Practice 2012, 13th ed., http://www.aph.gov.au/senate/pubs/odgers/index.htm, accessed 20 February 2013.

Office of Parliamentary Counsel 2008, Drafting Directive 4.10, 14 December, http://www.opc.gov.au/about/draft_directions.htm, accessed 20 February 2013.

Owens, M. 2012, 'Minister threatens Liberal leader', *The Australian*, 3 May.

Packham, B. 2013, 'ABC host Barrie Cassidy bows to Coalition, quitting government post to "avoid controversy"', *The Australian*, 25 October.

Prasser, S. 2012, 'Premier could care a bit more', *The Australian*, 2 February.

Proceedings of the Australian Constitutional Convention 26–29 April 1983, Vol. 1: appendix.

Queensland Government 2013, *Cabinet Handbook*, Queensland Government, Brisbane.

Reece, N. 2012, *Reflections on the Constitutional Issues Arising from Minority Australian Government 2010–2013*, Constitutional Conventions Workshop, University of Melbourne, 29–30 November.

Reid, G.S. 1977, 'Commentaries', in G. Evans (ed.), *Labor and the Constitution: Essays and Commentaries on Constitutional Controversies of the Whitlam Years in Australian Government*, Heinemann, Melbourne.

Reuters 1996, 'Queensland's Borbidge calls on Goss to go', Reuters News Service, 12 February.

Rhodes, R.A.W., Wanna, J. and Weller, P. 2009, *Comparing Westminster*, Oxford University Press, Oxford.

Rhodes, R.A.W. and Weller, P. 2005, 'Westminster transplanted and Westminster implanted: Exploring political change', in H. Patapan, J. Wanna and P. Weller (eds), *Westminster Legacies: Democracy and Responsible Government in Asia and the Pacific*, UNSW Press, Sydney.

Ross, M. 2013, 'Government accused of violating caretaker conventions over asylum seeker ad blitz', *ABC News*, 10 August.

Roy Morgan 2013, 'Roy Morgan Image of Professions Survey 2013', http://www.roymorgan.com/findings/image-of-professions-2013-201305020534, accessed 20 January 2014.

Sampford, C.J.G. 1987, '"Recognize and declare": An Australian experiment in codifying constitutional conventions', *Oxford Journal of Legal Studies*, 7(3), 369–420.

Sawer, M. 2006, 'Review of limiting democracy: The erosion of electoral rights in Australia', *Democratic Audit of Australia*, http://arts.anu.edu.au/democraticaudit/papers/20061006_sawer_review_ch_bc.pdf, accessed 20 February 2013.

Seccombe, M. and Allard, T. 2004, 'Hostage drama politicised, says ALP', *Sydney Morning Herald*, 16 September.

Sheridan, J. 2013, 'Caretaker 2013: Only talking business as usual', http://www.finance.gov.au/blog/2013/08/05/caretaker-2013-%E2%80%93-only-talking-business-usual, accessed 20 January 2014.

South Australia Department of the Premier and Cabinet (SADPC) 2013, *Caretaker Conventions and Pre-Election Practices: A Guide for South Australian Agencies*, SA Government, Adelaide.

Strangio, P. 2006, 'Incumbency dominance: An unhealthy trend?', Senate Occasional Lecture, 25 August.

Tasmanian Department of Premier & Cabinet (Tas DPC) 2014, *Guidelines on the Caretaker Conventions and the Operations of Government during the Caretaker Period*, Tasmanian Government, Hobart.

Taylor, J. 2013, 'NBN Co. enters caretaker mode', http://www.zdnet.com/au/nbn-co-enters-caretaker-mode-7000018950, accessed 20 January 2014.

Tiernan, A. 2007, *Power Without Responsibility: Ministerial Staffers in Australian Governments from Whitlam to Howard*. Sydney, UNSW Press, Sydney.

Tiernan, A. and Weller, P. 2010, *Learning to be a Minister: Heroic Expectations, Practical Realities*, Melbourne University Press, Melbourne.

Twomey, A. and Withers, G. 2007, *Federalist Paper 1: Australia's Federal Future*, report.

Victorian Department of Premier and Cabinet (Vic DPC) 2010, *Guidelines on the Caretaker Conventions: Guidance for Handling Government Business During the Election Period*, Victorian Government, Melbourne.

Wanna, J. 2006, 'Between a rock and hard place: The nonsense of Australia's *Charter of Budget Honesty Act 1998*', paper presented at Australasian Political Studies Association (ASPA) Conference, Newcastle, 25–27 September .

Wanna, J., Kelly, J. and Forster, J. 2000, *Managing Public Expenditure in Australia*, Allen & Unwin, Sydney.

Watt, I. 2013a, *Communication – 07 August 2013*, http://www.dpmc.gov.au/media/index.cfm#secretary, accessed 20 January 2014.

—— 2013b, *Communication – 06 August 2013*, http://www.dpmc.gov.au/media/index.cfm#secretary, accessed 20 January 2014.

—— 2013c, *Communication – 09 August 2013*, http://www.dpmc.gov.au/media/index.cfm#secretary, accessed 20 January 2014.

Weller, P. 2002, *Don't Tell the Prime Minister*, Scribe, Melbourne.

—— 2007, *Cabinet Government in Australia 1901–2006*, UNSW Press, Sydney.

Western Australian Department of Premier & Cabinet (WADPC) 2013, *Caretaker Conventions: Guidelines Applying in Western Australia During the State General Election Period*, Western Australian Government, Perth.

Wilson, J. 1995, 'Constitutional conventions and election campaigns: The status of the caretaker convention in Canada', *Canadian Parliamentary Review*, 18(4), 12.

Young, S. 2005, Submission to Joint Standing Committee on Electoral Matters Inquiry into the Conduct of the 2004 Federal Election and Matters Related Thereto, 4 May.

Appendix A. Different approaches – what the jurisdictional guidances say

This appendix collects and publishes for the first time all of the caretaker guidances from across Australia and New Zealand. This appendix collates and provides a brief overview of the similarities and differences of the approaches adopted by different jurisdictions.

In Australia, caretaker conventions were first published by the Commonwealth in 1987, although they had been explicitly articulated by prime ministers since 1951. The Commonwealth guidance is both the oldest and most authoritative—the majority of State provisions are derived from the Commonwealth. Since 1987, the tendency has been to add prescriptive detail and to enumerate the practices behind the conventions. Pressures on the management and interpretation of caretaker conventions discussed in chapter 5 have prompted a transition from the minimalist approach of a letter from Mr Menzies to his ministers, to a highly planned and administered process of updating and disseminating the caretaker conventions before an election, and providing advice on application during the election campaign.

All jurisdictions have engaged in an increased bureaucratisation of the process, with increased detail and advice in response to breaches and controversies. The focus of the New Zealand caretaker convention guidance, contained in *The Cabinet Manual*, is broader than its Australian counterparts because of that country's different electoral system. Introduction of the MMP system of voting in 1996 necessitated an increased focus on transitions and the formation of government. It contains detailed advice about procedures when it is not clear who will form the next government and on decision-making during an extended caretaker period. It was noted in Chapter 2 that in 1996 the caretaker period lasted for nine weeks. Although this has not been repeated at subsequent elections, New Zealand departments are encouraged to plan and prepare for the possibility of a protracted caretaker period (*The Cabinet Manual*, 2001 DPC, p. 58).

The emphases of caretaker guidance documents have shifted from advising ministers about appropriate conduct during the election period to supporting public sector officials to avoid perceptions of partisanship and prevent governments from exploiting the advantages of incumbency. The majority of jurisdictions now work with caretaker guidance documents that have dual objectives. Ministers and departmental officers have different roles during an election campaign and they need to be clear about their respective roles. As caretaker guidance documents become more detailed with prescriptive advice for public servants, there may be a need to develop and publish two guidances:

the first might be aimed at ministers, outlining their responsibilities within the broader Westminster context and reiterating their relationship with the public service during the caretaker period. The other would provide detailed advice for departments on how best to manage internal arrangements at a time when the fate of the Government is in the hands of the people, examples being the signing of correspondence or decisions about departmentally supported websites.

The State and Territory caretaker convention documents are available for downloading on the ANU Press website at http://press.anu.edu.au/titles/australia-and-new-zealand-school-of-government-anzsog-2/caretaker-conventions/.

www.ingramcontent.com/pod-product-compliance
Lightning Source LLC
Chambersburg PA
CBHW061241270326
41927CB00035B/3466